COME BACK TO EDEN
Lakeland's Northern Neighbour

John Hurst

For Dulcie,
another lover of Eden,
and others near and dear

Published by Sigma Leisure – an imprint of
Sigma Press, 1 South Oak Lane, Wilmslow, Cheshire SK9 6AR, England.

British Library Cataloguing in Publication Data
A CIP record for this book is available from the British Library.

ISBN: 1-85058-705-1

Typesetting and Design by: Sigma Press, Wilmslow, Cheshire.

Cover Design: Design House

Cover photographs: The town centre of Appleby, showing St Lawrence's Church and the Moot Hall, meeting place of the town council *(Frederick C. Wilson)*; red squirrels like this scamper about the woodlands of Eden *(NPI Red Alert)*; judging sheep at the village show at Kaber, near Kirkby Stephen *(Wayne Hutchinson)*; the morning mist rises from the surface of Ullswater on a sublime day in September *(John Hurst)*.

Printed by: MFP Design & Print

Preface

As you descend from the heights of Hartside or motor down the gentler decline of Stainmore, a vast panorama of the Cumbrian countryside, dotted with villages and small towns, stretches out ahead – the glorious carpet of the Eden Valley. Not many outsiders know a great deal about this delectable part of northern England, although millions enthuse about the neighbouring lands of the Lake District, so rich in breathtaking mountains and waterways.

The appeal of Eden lies in a gentler, more subtle brand of beauty, typified by well-tended farmland, tranquil villages like Ormside and Warcop, Great Salkeld and Kirkoswald, and spectacular vistas which embrace both the sweep of the valley and the majesty of distant fells, be they the smooth-topped Pennines, to the east, or the more rugged Lakeland hills, to the west.

Eden offers some panoramic plums, such as the magnificence of the vast view down the valley which can be seen from the winding road above the village of Kaber, near Kirkby Stephen, preferably in high summer. Smaller snapshots of appeal make us stop and stare. A lively cluster of children on a village green, waiting their turns at an ice-cream van, perhaps, or sheepdogs at work on a craggy hillside, or the view across the Eden at Appleby, with a clutter of hungry ducks in the foreground, pestering passers-by, and cricketers at play on the greensward beyond the far bank.

Stray thoughts float into the memory, most of them from a past era. Perhaps the fleeting vision is of an old-style bobby pounding his rural beat; the sight of newly-turned, chocolate-coloured earth, as ploughman and horse trudge across a field, hungry seagulls dipping low into the fresh furrows; a postman astride a pushbike, handing letters over a garden wall; a village showfield, full of activity and colour, with men and women in their "Sunday best"; or wind-driven rain angling down in silent, repetitive waves, in harmony with the rise and fall of gusts, shimmering against the sombre backcloth of a mountainside.

Thousands of mini-memories crowd into the thoughts. Native

Cumbrians, of the Eden Valley and other parts, are seen as stolid, unappreciative types. The truth is that, with so much natural beauty all around them, so much grandeur and fascination, they see no need for outbursts of enthusiasm. Leave that to visiting strangers.

The essential Eden lies in the valley through which the river flows, although it also gives its name to a wider, but still distinctive part of east Cumbria, including Alston Moor, in the Pennines, Shap Fell and some of North Lakeland, all within the empire of the Penrith-based Eden District Council since local government reorganisation drew them together in 1974.

The official view is that this latter Eden is almost paradise. The Central Statistical Office made a survey in 1992, containing hundreds of comparisons between contrasting parts of the country. One of the striking revelations was that Eden was the most sparsely populated district, with just 35 people to the square mile, comparing dramatically with the 18,657 crammed into a similar area of a London borough. On this basis, a researcher described Eden as "the closest thing to Paradise in the whole country".

I have lived in Eden or, to be precise, its "capital", Penrith, for more than 60 years. As an addict, I have decided to write about the aspects of the place which I find appealing, partly out of a desire to record some of the changes I have seen and partly – probably primarily – as a kind of deep-felt appreciation of feelings of privilege and pleasure in having been able to live and work in this special place.

This backward glance at the Eden Valley of yesteryear is largely based on impressions and observations accumulated during more than half-a-century as a journalist working for the area's weekly newspaper. The Penrith-based *Cumberland and Westmorland Herald* is also the main repository of many of the facts and photographs which appear on the pages which follow.

My thanks are due to the men who took the pictures, Alec Fraser, Eric Davidson, Frederick C. Wilson, Harry Brookes, Fred Horrobin, John T. Hall, John Jameson, Wayne Hutchinson, NPI Red Alert and Gordon Wood. I also acknowledge, with sincere thanks, the help given by colleagues David Bracken and Nancy Stonehouse in preparing this text.

Now, come back to Eden...

John Hurst

Contents

1

Eden threesome

Civil servants, with local government in mind, consulted a map of the old counties of Cumberland and Westmorland and drew a bold line around a vast area of countryside, dotted with small towns and villages. Whether by chance or by a masterstroke of creative genius it cannot be said, but in the early-1970s the result was the new garden of Eden.

Unwittingly, perhaps, the planners produced a threesome of scenic delights, with the Valley of the Eden river lying in luxuriant splendour between two immense tracts of contrasting beauty and appeal – the rolling mountains and moors of the Pennines, to the east, and the lushness of Lakeland around Ullswater, to the west.

In the beginning, the district was given the prosaic title of No. 3 District of Cumbria, awaiting the choice of a suitable name, a fascinating business which was left to the natives. "Wanted: A new name for No. 3 District," said a headline in the *Herald*. The response was immediate and varied, and suggestions came from London, Kent and Essex, as well as from within the district. They ranged from the semi-acceptable, like West Pennine, Cross Fell, Eden Dales and Westmorland (the old county title) to the nonsensical and the concocted, such as Wordsworth Vale, Walpole St Hugh, Herrieslink, Coleridge County, Peneden, Heraldshire and Penappmoor (the latter advanced because it incorporated parts of Penrith, Appleby and Alston Moor).

In the opinion of the Department of the Environment, the name should be simple and straightforward, rather than hybrid or double-barrelled. At a joint meeting of the old councils, due to fade out under reorganisation, one of the North Westmorland Council members, Mrs. M. Sowerby, from the village of Winton, proposed Eden – after the river.

The short, simple name was both apt and appealing. The river began at the head of Mallerstang, within a mile of the district boundary, said Mrs. Sowerby, and it flowed through the vale to Appleby, where the valley widened and lesser rivers, the Lyvennet, the Lowther and the Eamont (out of Ullswater) became tributaries. The suggested title was adopted with acclaim, for Eden symbolized the "delectable land" described by Mrs Sowerby.

So delectable, in fact, that the valley has since been declared a Site of Special Scientific Interest. On one side is a breathtaking stretch of the Lake District National Park, centred on Ullswater, and on the other lies Alston Moor, a ravishing wilderness now entitled an Area of Outstanding Natural Beauty. All this in one official package – it is a rare mix. Inevitably, Penrith became the headquarters of the new council and there was recognition, in the name, of the placid towns and clusters of villages spread around the valley.

One of the smaller towns, Appleby, nestles below its historic hill-top castle, in a loop of the Eden which holds the old place closely, rather like a lover's possessive cuddle. Trickling, flowing or surging – its moods differ according to the seasons – the river gives Appleby lustre and appeal. It seems almost obligatory for people passing through to stop and park their cars by the side of the watercourse, on The Sands, feed the ducks on the near bank or gaze dreamily across the Eden to the cricket ground beyond.

The cricket field, or Vicarage Croft, is one of the visual delights, especially if there happens to be a match in progress and the sun is sparkling through the surrounding trees. The river drifts past one of the boundaries, while another runs alongside the churchyard of St Lawrence's. In a bygone age, whenever a funeral took place, the cricket was suspended and players stood reverently, with heads uncovered, until the cortege departed. Other hold-ups were caused when burly batsmen lofted six-hits into the river and the ball had to be recovered, with the aid of a long net. In recent years the field has been threatened by would-be developers. Thankfully, their advances have so far been resisted, for Appleby would not be Appleby without this sublime setting for sport.

A toast to Henry II was drunk by people of Appleby in July 1979 at a pageant to mark the 800th anniversary of granting the charter of the town. One of the leading parts was taken by the Mayor of Appleby, Mr Reg Folder (second from left).

In the sweet summer time the Eden ripples over the shallows and glides along the pools. But when goaded by a sudden tempest it can burst from its fastness among the mountains of Mallerstang, at the head of the valley, and dash down with the force of a cataract, sweeping away everything movable in its path, sheep and cattle included. When the wild rage is spent, the river settles down again between its banks and meanders peacefully, as though nothing untoward has happened.

The spring of 1968 saw two such terrible days when the turbulent waters, in full volume, descended on Appleby. The old town, crowned by its castled height, rose out of the water like a second Venice. That was the unforgettable weekend when the main disaster occurred further downstream, near the village of Langwathby, where the torrent caused chaos by sweeping away an old stone bridge which carried the main Penrith-Alston road. Meanwhile, the folk of Appleby fought a losing battle in trying to prevent water from gushing into homes, shops and pubs as the river burst its banks. Television news bulletins carried spectacular film of floods closing the A66, which ran through the town, and submerging big areas of land, including the cricket field. Any repetition of the drama of 1968 has been made unlikely by the installation of a flood defence system.

There are more than 900 years of lively history behind Appleby Castle, perched on an eminence above the town and the river – years of battle and bloodshed when it was attacked by Scottish raiders, years of greater style and colour when it was the home of Lady Anne Clifford, Countess of Dorset and Pembroke, and daughter of Queen Elizabeth's champion, the Earl of Cumberland. Under the influence of this "great wise woman", castles and churches were rescued from ruin and new buildings were added, including almshouses at Appleby, close to the castle gates. Her name is still revered in the Eden Valley, although she died over 300 years ago.

The dominance of the castle used to extend far beyond the boundaries of the town, for the castle estate embraced 20,000 acres of the valley – grouse moors, farms and commons – as well as many Appleby houses, shops and an inn. History turned a corner in 1962, following the death of Lord Hothfield, with the break-up of the estate, including the sale of the castle itself to Liverpool businessman John Coney.

The castle filled a dual role when it next changed hands in the 1970s. Denis Vernon, as chairman of Ferguson Industrial Holdings, used it as a management training centre but also contributed to the local tourism effort by conserving rare breeds of wildfowl, sheep and Vietnamese pot-bellied pigs. The ancient keep became a falconry. The castle continues to fascinate visitors, though its ownership changed during the 1990s.

Appleby, though remaining a proud little town, was shorn of three distinctions in the space of four years, the first of them in 1970 when Westmorland Assizes were held for the last time, after seven centuries.

The former Westmorland was not the most criminal or violent of the old shire counties and the judges, who presided at Appleby in the austere setting of the Shire Hall, were often presented with

Light snow and ice gave a lustre to the town centre of Appleby as the Lunesdale foxhounds set out. In the background are St Lawrence's church and its cloisters.

white gloves by the high sheriff to mark the fact that there were no cases of serious crime – although civil proceedings for breaches of promises to marry could add spice to the sittings.

The assizes, generally held twice a year, gave a sense of splendour and importance to the town. Peals rang out from the bells of St Lawrence's Church as the judge was driven slowly through the streets, originally in a stately coach, and later in a shining Rolls Royce, escorted by policemen on foot and headed by uniformed trumpeters. Bewigged counsel filled the well of the court as the clerk of assize solemnly read the Queen's Commission of "Oyer and Terminer and General Gaol Delivery".

It seemed that Westmorland and Appleby paid a penalty because they were not lawless enough. At the last assizes in 1970, Judge Brabin offered words of consolation: "Appleby has not experienced the growth and the influx of people that other places have. It has not, therefore, experienced the increase in crime. Although Appleby has lost its assizes, it has kept so much that when a balance is struck, it may be thought that, in view of what has been retained, the forfeiture paid is worthwhile."

Sadly, officialdom struck again at the imposing image of Appleby during the semi-turmoil of local government reorganisation in 1974 – sweeping alterations which played havoc with the map of old England by merging, chopping and changing.

The former sister counties of Cumberland and Westmorland were drawn together and, with part of what had been North Lancashire and a fragment of Yorkshire, the far-reaching new county of Cumbria was formed. Feelings ran high in Appleby which, under the former regime, held the title of county town of Westmorland. In a splendid show of traditionalism, largely inspired by Martin Holmes, a local historian, councillors achieved a name-change to Appleby-in-Westmorland to ensure preservation of the old title. But the former status was gone.

Of five lesser authorities which were supplanted by reorganisation in the new Eden district, the grandest by far – though not the largest – was Appleby Borough Council. Councillors continue to look splendid in their robes, whenever they meet in the picturesque Moot Hall, now reduced in power to the level of a parish council – though a lot of pride still prevails on mayor-making day.

Appleby boasts twelve royal charters, the first dated 1179. In centuries past the local establishment included not only a mayor, aldermen and councillors, but a coroner, serjeant at mace, two chamberlains, three aletasters, four sealers and searchers of leather, three swine-lookers and several hedge-lookers. The greatest honour an Applebian could aspire to was that of being elected a freeman of the borough, a distinction which was erased by the changes of 1974.

Being a councillor in old-time Appleby must have demanded a hearty appetite and a degree of durability, for the calendar included extravagant junketing and fulsome speeches. When Lord Hothfield, as mayor, hosted a dinner in 1896, the newspapers printed the full menu: **Soups** – hare, oyster. **Fish** – turbot, anchovy sauce; cod, oyster sauce. **Joints** – Sirloin beef, roast mutton, boiled mutton, roast geese, roast turkey, boiled chickens, Cumberland hams, venison, caper sauce, pheasants, partridges. **Sweets** – Plum puddings, cabinet pudding, tart, tartlets, cheese cakes, apricot jellies and creams, trifle, dessert.

With the mountain of food disposed of, guests settled down to listen to an awesome toast list: The Queen ... The Prince and Princess of Wales and the rest of the Royal family ... HM Forces on land and sea ... Lord Lieutenant and magistrates of the county ... The Bishop and clergy and ministers of all denominations ... the mayor ... the council of the borough ... prosperity to the town and trade ... agricultural interests ... chairman ... vice-chairman ... the press ... visitors ... ladies.

In another departure from tradition, Appleby also lost the splendour of the marching bands and fluttering banners, the gaiety of Punch and Judy shows, swings and roundabouts, the football and sports of the annual demonstration of the Vale of Eden Band of Hope Union. For more than a century, it was one of the summer highlights of the Eden Valley, alternating between two sites – the Broad Close at Appleby and the Hills Bottom at Kirkby Stephen.

The stage was set for advocates of total abstinence, including specialist speakers of the North of England Temperance League, to put across their messages – and they certainly pulled no punches. Speeches were spiced with phrases like "the evils of drink", the "cursed traffic" and "licensed temptation".

The rest of the day was devoted to fun and enjoyment, providing a rare opportunity for country children to see marionette shows, conjurors and ventriloquists, while their parents relaxed and listened to brass bands, hopefully in the sunshine. Although the demonstration ceased as an annual event in the 1990s, the Band of Hope Union aimed to protect the youth of Eden from temptation until falling numbers led to its wind-up in 2000.

An emotive dilemma has plagued the small market town of Kirkby Stephen, springing from its situation astride the road which connects two of the busiest routes in northern England – the M6 motorway and the A66 Penrith-Scotch Corner road. While shopkeepers have welcomed the boost to trade, the sheer volume of traffic has put mounting pressure on Kirkby Stephen's single main street, leading to an explosive debate and persistent calls for a bypass of the town or, failing that, some form of ban on heavy goods vehicles.

Such heated controversy seems out of place in a chummy, easy-going town. Kirkby Stephen sits at the centre of the agricultural lands of Upper Eden, provides farmers with supplies and sells their livestock through its auction mart. Record prices are paid for Swaledale rams at the three-day sales every October.

The infant Eden flows close to the town – so close that, if you know your way through the network of lanes and alleyways, you can leave the Kirkby Stephen market square and be relaxing beside the river in two or three minutes.

Each October Kirkby Stephen took on a rodeo-like atmosphere as horses and ponies, which had been grazing on the nearby fells, were driven through the town centre, heading for the annual Cowper Day sale at the auction mart. They made a fine sight but the spectacular drive was stopped after a fatality in 1964 when a 12-year-old local boy died after a fall from a pony.

Take a walk up the steeply-sloping main street of Alston, listening to snatches of gossip and shouted greetings. The impression created by the native twang is that you could be in a small town on Tyneside, in the North-East of England, rather than a remote outpost of the Eden district where the distinctive Cumbrian dialect prevails.

For Alston's association with Eden is primarily a local government association. In the reshuffle of local authorities of 1974, Alston-with-Garrigill Rural Council disappeared and the Eden District Council took over responsibility for the town and its environs.

While Appleby and Kirkby Stephen nestle cosily in the valley below, Alston is perched high in the Pennines, springing up sharply from a dip in the hilly land where the South Tyne flows. The approach to the little town from the heartland of Eden is by way of a climbing, winding road, flanked by the dramatic expanses of Hartside and Alston Moor. Already remote, Alston becomes even more solitary in the depths of winter when fierce winds drift snow across Hartside Pass and other high roads.

The town has so much olde-worlde quaintness, even uniqueness, that its main street has been used as a setting for period films. The road surface of stone setts seems more in keeping with the age of the horse and cart than with the cars which now pass through the town, some stopping so that visitors, enamoured by the appeal of the place, can visit pubs, cafes or antique shops.

The story is still told in Alston of how horses played a part in the defence of the countryside during the 1939-45 war. When the Home

Horses from Appleby New Fair, held each June, are often taken for a dip in the Eden.
(Frederick Cameron Wilson)

Guard was formed, cart horses, plough horses and dales ponies were also enlisted and the town platoon became one of the few mounted units in Britain. The terrain of rolling hills and stretching valleys could not be covered on foot, so the horses and ponies were ridden by the part-time soldiers – mainly farmers and shepherds – who went on patrol in riding breeches, cavalry puttees and bandoliers slung across their shoulders.

There was another example of Alston initiative in 1975 when British Rail closed the railway line which linked the town with Haltwhistle. It was a worrying loss to a remote community but they turned it to their advantage by developing a stretch of the picturesque track into a narrow gauge line, which is run by the South Tynedale Railway Preservation Society, and trips upon it are a considerable tourism attraction.

Long gone are the days when Alston Moor depended heavily on lead mining, with hundreds of men employed by the Vieille Montagne Company. A new age dawned when the company ended its operations in 1949, although old mines have been converted into symbolic reminders of the industrial past to contribute to the economy of the future.

Ullswater moved Wordsworth to write his poignant poem about its daffodils and Cecil Spring-Rice to pen the stirring words of "I vow to thee my country", later put to music as a patriotic song by Gustav Holst. Much more was written about her charms in 1961-62 when Cumbrians, in particular, rose in opposition to fend off Manchester's unacceptable first effort to turn the lake into a source of water supply. "As a sterile reservoir, Ullswater would be no use to anyone except the thirsty people of Manchester," wrote *Herald* editor George Hobley.

The *Daily Telegraph* columnist, Peter Simple, joined in the opposition: "Myself, I am ready to sit down on the banks of Ullswater for months on end, if necessary. And even if nobody else will sit with me, I shall know that the great shades of Wordsworth and Coleridge, Ruskin and Arnold, are at my side."

Thousands signed petition forms as resistance to the Manchester plan mounted. The campaign culminated in a crescendo of fine words in the House of Lords when Lord Birkett of Ulverston delivered the finishing blow to Manchester's hopes, pleading that Ullswater should not suffer the same fate as Thirlmere and Haweswater – "both lovely lakes which have now been murdered ... now dead reservoirs, with no human life and sterile shores".

By 70 votes to 36, the waterworks clauses relating to Ullswater were deleted from the Manchester Corporation Bill, but the joy was muted through a tragic anti-climax – the death of Lord Birkett who was struck down within 48 hours of his great triumph of advocacy. A fell near the lake was named after him as a tribute to his vital role in the defeat of the plan.

Two years later Manchester again sought water, but this time the scheme was not seen as a threat to natural beauty and the city got its supply – "unseen and unheard", with water pumped under dividing fells to Haweswater, already a reservoir, seven miles away.

Before the M6 motorway reached Cumbria, Ullswater was a much remoter, even coy lake, drawing fewer admirers than Windermere and Grasmere, at the heart of the "honeypot" of Lakeland. In 1955 it "hit the headlines" when it was chosen by Donald Campbell, the speed ace, for an attempt on the world water speed record in his new version of "Bluebird", a £25,000 turbo-jet hydroplane. Excitement gripped the normally placid lakeshore, as big crowds assembled to watch the day-by-day build-up to the vital run, completed at a triumphant 202.32 mph.

This was hailed as a memorable achievement but – allied to increased use by water-skiers – it aroused fears that the precious lake might lose its atmosphere of quiet contemplation. A ban on speeding motorboats eased the doubts about a change of character.

Penrith is not only the "capital" of the administrative district of Eden but, also, the only town of any appreciable size, a historical place with strong agricultural associations, which lies at the cross-roads of Cumbria, the joining-point of the M6 motorway with the A66, from east to west, and the A6, once the primary north-south route.

The opening of the Penrith bypass section of the M6, in 1968, did much more than remove the din, stink and nuisance of grinding queues of heavy traffic from the middle of the old market town. Developers favoured the south-west fringe of town, close to the motorway, an area which now contains a posh hotel, the auction mart, a visitor centre, a massive market each Saturday and other business and Environment Agency premises – where once there were pleasant walks, scuttling rabbits, grazing cattle and birdsong.

The noisy bustle of the Saturday market, in particular, has introduced the cosmopolitan into the heart of the countryside. What was once a blissful rural scene is transformed by jostling crowds and avenues of stalls offering everything from cheap meat to chocolate, lavatory cleansers to ladies' briefs, bedsheets to break-fasts-in-bread-rolls.

Changes are inevitable – but old memories linger on.

2

Growing up...

In less sophisticated days, long before children were given computers, we had simple pastimes and pleasures, all with unaccountable seasons. Suddenly, and for no apparent reason, the marbles would appear. Boys everywhere would be playing, by the roadside and in school playgrounds, flicking the shiny, brightly-painted earthenware balls and the more coveted glass ones with colourful spiral centres. Chubby, grubby hands spanned prodigious distances – not always, perhaps, with prodigious honesty – to augment collections of marbles which numbered in scores, even hundreds.

The calendar of boyhood was a fluid one. Inexplicably, marbles would go out of fashion. Hoops (or boolies) would take their place – wooden ones propelled by a short stick, or iron ones trundled along with a hook, which enabled agile manipulators to perform remarkable evolutions.

So it went on. Kites, tops and whips, roller skates and other forms of youthful amusement all took their turns at undetermined times. The exception, of course, was the seasonal arrival of "conkers" which, of necessity, dominated playtimes when horse chestnuts were at their shiny prime on trees near to towns and villages.

Meanwhile, small girls indulged in their own speciality of hopscotch, played with flat stones on chalked footpaths. If some refreshment was needed in the middle of all the exertions, it might possibly be from a shaking bottle (or "shacky" bottle) containing an unwholesome-looking mixture of water and liquorice, a popular home-made drink in the days before cans of Coca-Cola dominated.

"Gis a swig o' thi shacky bottle," was a demand sometimes heard among gangs of children.

Wartime rationing restricted the other juvenile treats like chocolate and sweets. In pre-war days, however, anybody with a penny or a ha'penny could visit Harry Pattinson's little shop at the top of Castlegate, Penrith, and choose from a rich variety – gobstoppers, liquorice shoelaces, barley sugar sticks, sherbet dabs and Devon cream toffee bars among them.

Many children of past generations enjoyed the sugary sticks sold by James ("Candy") Barnes, a Penrith-born man, who regularly attended agricultural shows, sports meetings and farm sales, to which he walked many miles with a tin box of goodies hanging from his shoulders. There was nothing of the loud-voiced street hawker about the man, as he made people aware of his presence with the quiet but crisp announcement, "Candy, candy".

Among other stray memories of childhood there is a vivid one of short-panted boys, armed with jam jars, setting out across fields on the edge of towns and villages. Their destinations were watering places, such as the Horse Shoe pond, near to Penrith, where clusters of jelly-like frogspawn lay on muddy surfaces. The stuff held a strange fascination for children in the 1930s and 40s, who took it home by the jarful so that they could observe the development of full-blown tadpoles. In the fullness of time, tiny frogs would emerge but by then most children had been ordered to return their "catches" to the pond.

Horse Shoe pond was one of the countryside features which disappeared completely in the mid-1960s when contractors cut a swathe across the fields just to the west of Penrith, the route of the M6 of the future. Many other pastimes made up the ritual of childhood: climbing trees, clambering over rough field walls, damming streams, racing dogs, sticks and catapults, picking mushrooms and plucking brambles were all parts of being a child with lush countryside as a playground.

More orthodox games like football could be tricky, with tufts of grass and occasional cowpats to impede running, dribbling and shooting, as our 'Wembley' was generally in a farmer's field. Referees were unknown at this level of rustic soccer and verbal outbursts could be loud and rude as centre forwards squabbled with defenders about the validity of "goals", which were always open to question when jackets or overcoats represented the goalposts.

Whatever the scoreline after two hours or so, the cry went up: "Next goal's the winner". Efforts were briefly renewed until the ball went whizzing between the heaps of clothing once again.

When we put down our playthings we turned to the picture houses, the "flicks", for those were the great days of the silver screen, with *real* stars like Clark Gable, James Cagney and James Mason, Bette Davis, Joan Fontaine, Greer Garson and Joan Crawford. Some, however, preferred the robust humour of Old Mother Riley or the profound detective powers of Charlie Chan.

There was a time – and, strangely, it doesn't seem long ago – when Penrith nightlife centred on its cinemas, the Alhambra and the Regent. Stars of Hollywood could also be seen at the Cosy at Appleby, the Gem at Shap, a nameless cinema at Kirkby Stephen, or by means of a mobile cinema which enabled villagers in places like Brough, Kirkoswald and Dufton to view some of the old classics.

As each of the town cinemas generally put on two films per week, moviegoers were guaranteed a feast of entertainment, rich in romance, glamour, mirth and mystery, song and dance. In the course of a week, Penrith people could relish a Will Hay comedy, a war-time drama with Humphrey Bogart and the sinister Peter Lorre, a John Wayne western and then flit back to the lighthearted through the daftness of George Formby who repeatedly found himself in crazy situations but always came up smiling as he strummed his ukelele. "Turned out nice again . . . "

Many youngsters gathered in one of the milkbars to decide which of the Penrith cinemas to patronise and whether their finances would stretch to a seat in the circle or merely in the back stalls. We could not leave it too late because there were always queues for the second house, starting just after 8 o'clock. Then, for two hours or more, we were whisked away from rationing, short-ages and other post-war frustrations into a world of make-believe: a world in which good always triumphed over evil, the "bad guy" was unmasked in the last reel, the hero got his girl and the US Cavalry, with bugles blaring, arrived in the nick of time to save the wagon train from hordes of bloodthirsty red Indians.

Romance blossomed both on and off the screen. Young love was recognised at the Regent by the provision of double seats on the back row; they were in great demand. Teenage "love affairs" seldom amounted to more than innocent hand-holding or persistent smooching. However harmless, they were well publicised by scribblings on public buildings and elsewhere. The register of romantic pairings took the form of initials: L.S. = P.M. ... J.L.= D.M. ... T.R = R.A. ... and so on through a large percentage of the juvenile populace.

Just walk with a girl in the rose garden of the town park, or be seen together outside a cinema, and the association could be recorded among the messy scars on the pavilion in the park or even on the inside wall of a public lavatory: "P.S. loves D.K. True, by one who knows". One popular girl listed her conquests by writing the numerous boyfriends' initials on the whitened mudguards of her bicycle!

"If music be the food of love, play on ...". Dances were an integral part of social life, certainly for younger folk. Long before the days of blaring pop music and discos, the atmosphere was rather more tranquil and refined. Village halls throbbed with the music of the fox-trot, waltz and quickstep, ending with the inviting strains of "Who's taking you home tonight?", played by Jackson's band from Thirlmere, Bowman's from Cockermouth, the Blue Star band, the Lonsdale orchestra, Alan Strong's full accordion band or some other. The identity of the musicians mattered little; much of the inducement was romance and the hope of a walk with somebody in the moonlight.

At two shillings (10p) or half-a-crown (12½p) for four hours, village dances, hunt balls, farmers' balls or old-time dances were superb value. Sometimes the bus proprietors at Appleby and Penrith ran 'specials' to take townies to and from the more popular ones. For young Penrithians of the fifties, a visit to the "bop hop" at the Drill Hall on Saturday night was almost obligatory. The feeling was that, as members of a communal family, the Drill Hall was the place to be after a few drinks at one of the pubs. The soothing tones of Frank Walton and his Melody Makers made it even more irresistible.

Socialising, whether in the dance hall, the milkbar, the cinema or the YMCA, was spiced with the Cumbrian dialect which, as the years pass, is gradually being eradicated by the silky perfection of BBC announcers and other television-based influences. For the time being, though, the local language persists in pockets of resistance to change, depending largely on the company you are in. Talking to a stranger, we drop the dialect, but, if we meet a very old friend, it's different: "Noo then, Fred. Ista still hingin' on? Better than some, though."

In those far-off days the word 'gay' was not outlawed because of associations with homosexuality. Cumbrians used the expression in dialect, as in sentences like:

"Ah telt him he wad hev ta be gay quick ... "

"Ah went down Doctor's Brow at a gay clatter on me bike ... "

"Ah hope thoos gaily weel ... "

"Ah hed a gay scufter ta git theer on time ... "

A newspaper report of a trip to the capital to watch a bowling competition was headlined, "A gay day in London".

True Cumbrians, men and women, who have grown up with the dialect since infancy, and heard elderly relatives relishing it, never forget nor totally abandon the language of their county. They simply pick their time to give voice to it: "Canny oald Cummerlan' caps them aw still ... "

Sadly, childhood and teenage years were all that some of our companions knew of their native county. Job opportunities were limited and, although some youngsters of the 1940s and 1950s found work in auctioneering, the police, local government, education, local shops and offices, bonds were broken with others who were forced to leave the immediate area to make a future for themselves. Young farmers were more fortunate, in that they inherited holdings, but agriculture also faced a degree of uncertainty; with the increase in mechanisation, small farms were merged into bigger ones and, as the years advanced, there was a slow-but-sure reduction in farms and in openings for younger men and women. The drift from the land gathered pace.

3

Eden at war

The battle of Penrith began at dusk on Saturday, 5th September 1942. A newspaper account, headed "Penrith invaded", recalls the build-up to hostilities. England had been invaded a week earlier and the German forces had fought their way from the east and over the Pennines, heading towards the A6 Carlisle to Shap road.

Ready and waiting for the challenge were men of the Home Guard, Penrith's wartime garrison, alongside civil defence volunteers of the ARP. Fighting went on throughout the night, first beside the River Eden and then in the streets of Penrith. Twice the town was bombed from the air and severe casualties were sustained before the enemy finally over-ran the railway station and nearby Penrith Castle.

Happily, this realistic exercise – for exercise it was – proved to be the closest Penrith ever came to front-line action in the war of 1939-45 (apart from the jettisoning of a bomb in open countryside, a few miles to the south of the town). The aim of the trial was to test the degree of co-operation of all services – military, police and civil defence – as the team concerned in the defence of a key town.

Incidents were made as effective as possible, although the safety of the population was uppermost. Thunderflashes, crackers and blank ammunition threatened the sleep but not the lives of townsfolk. A group of women, enjoying an evening out, suddenly found themselves embroiled in the mock battle and had to be smuggled into Penrith through the defences, with the enemy advancing in close pursuit.

The "battle" of 1942 was one of several exercises which dotted the war years in Penrith and the rest of Cumbria. As early as November 1939 the town was "bombed", an imaginary attack to test novice ARP wardens and VAD personnel who manned first-aid posts in church halls. Pupils of the grammar school masqueraded as casualties and lay on the sawdust-covered floor of the auction mart, each tagged with a label to indicate the nature of the "injuries" he had sustained, for there wasn't a spot of blood to be seen. I sustained "multiple facial injuries" and my head was swathed in bandages as I was moved to a first aid post in St Andrew's church hall with others.

One of the closest approaches to the "real thing" was in the town's Norfolk Road where Sergt. McAully, a police officer trained in ARP work, created a room from corrugated sheeting and old furniture, ignited it with an incendiary bomb and showed onlookers how to fight the flames with a stirrup hand pump. Many Cumbrian air-raid sirens were never sounded "in anger" but were regularly tested to ensure that they were in working order.

Back to 1939. The nation braced itself for war long before Prime Minister Chamberlain's fateful pronouncement. While young men enlisted in the Territorial Army, older ones trained to be ARP wardens. "Be prepared," said a newspaper advertisement in mid-1939. "Be prepared. Have your blinds and curtains ready for a black-out. We have special ARP curtain fabrics in black, green, brown and blue at three shillings per yard. Also, a special fabric which has been tested and found satisfactory against gas, tear gas, phosgene and chlorine."

Like the fabric advertisers, N. Arnison and Sons, the Penrith drapers, most folk seemed to be in little doubt that, sooner or later, the peacefulness of the Cumbrian countryside would be shattered by the horror of war. We wanted to believe the Prime Minister's prediction of "peace in our time" but could not convince ourselves.

At the final of the Waitby Cup, the Upper Eden Valley football competition, in 1939, the excitement of the play was overshadowed by the growing likelihood of war and the probability that before the next final, players and spectators would be "called up" into HM Forces. The first gas masks arrived, in their cardboard containers, and initial steps were taken to find homes for young evacuees, due to arrive as soon as war broke out.

The tranquillity of the 1930s was finally shattered when Chamberlain announced: "The German Chancellor has not hesitated to plunge the world into misery to serve his own senseless ambitions."

URGENT NOTICE.

AIR RAIDS.

IMPORTANT MEETINGS

will be held as under:

On Sunday, 26th January.

KESWICK, THE ALHAMBRA, at 11 a.m.
PENRITH, THE ALHAMBRA at 2-30 p.m.
COCKERMOUTH, PUBLIC HALL, at 8 p.m.

All Members of A.R.P., A.F.S., H.G., W.V.S., First Aid and other Services should attend.

SPEAKERS WITH FIRST-HAND KNOWLEDGE OF THE "BLITZED" TOWNS WILL TELL HOW TO MEET THE ATTACK.

GEO. HARRISON, Hon. Secretary,
Federation of Cumberland Information Committee.

The trauma of the announcement, on 3rd September 1939, began a momentous period which etched itself on the memories of all who lived through the war years – Dunkirk ... the Battle of Britain ... North Africa ... the D-Day landings ... the joy and emotion of the VE and VJ celebrations.

Although precise memories may have faded somewhat, the war sparked words and phrases which always come to mind when we think of 1939-45: ration books ... respirators (or gas masks) ... black-out ... ARP ... clothing coupons ... digging for victory ... Home Guard ... "Careless talk costs lives" ... evacuees ... air-raid shelters ... sirens ... identity cards ... "Some chicken, some neck" ... Tobruk ... Pearl Harbour ... "Eat more potatoes" ... war savings ... land girls ... "war ag" committees ... Bevin boys ... conscientious objectors ...

In the last pre-war issues of weekly newspapers there were accounts and results of traditional events like the agricultural show in the pretty parish of Crosby Ravensworth. That was virtually the cessation of typical summer-time gatherings, for the next issues told of the cancellation of the shows at Shap, Ousby and Nenthead and of a missionary sale at Dacre. Sadly, some of the events ended peremptorily by the war of 1939, were never to be revived when peace returned. The show at Shap, for instance.

The immediate prospects appeared to be grim. Emergency announcements pub-

PUBLIC NOTICES .

Joint Committee for Soviet Aid

RED ARMY FLAG DAY

will be held in PENRITH on

Saturday, 19th February.

PLEASE HELP THE WOUNDED.

lished in the local papers suggested that the realities of war would soon be upon the fair counties of Cumberland and Westmorland:

* All cinemas were to be closed.
* People must keep off the streets as much as possible. By exposing themselves unnecessarily, they would add to the danger. They should also make sure that their gas masks fitted.
* Boy Scouts were deemed to be on "national duty" and should wear their uniforms at all times.
* Householders must turn off their gas supplies if there was an air-raid.
* Air raids would be signalled by sirens, by hooters and by blasts on police whistles. Hand rattles would be used should there be a gas attack.

These measures might work in the towns but how could people in remote places be aroused to the threat of a bombing attack? Villagers of Garrigill, in the Pennines, near Alston, had a unique warning device, a big bass drum which was to be beaten in the main street in the event of an alert. The drum, something of an antique, formerly used by a village band, remained in the custody of a resident until it was sold by public auction in 1972.

The first major impact of war on Cumbrian towns and villages was the arrival of evacuees, mainly schoolchildren from the North-East, thought to be under threat from aerial attacks. Enduring links were formed as a result of their residence with hosts and hostesses over a wide area of what is now Cumbria, then the counties of Cumberland and Westmorland.

"Penrith seems to have been fortunate in its evacuated guests. 850 blue-blazered boys now throng the streets, well disciplined, respectful and anxious to lend a hand," wrote Tom Sarginson, *Herald* editor, in September 1939, following the arrival in town of the pupils of Newcastle Royal Grammar School, who spent the war years with Penrith families. The town not only provided homes for the boys but the arrival of some 400 others, teachers, officials and parents, meant that every scrap of empty property was snapped up. The main cause for concern, arising from the influx, was the strain on the town's water supply, then dependent solely on Hayeswater, in the Lakeland fells. The urban council published notices calling for the greatest possible economy, as there were 1,300 additional thirsts to slake.

The "invasion" from Newcastle made a big impact on education in Penrith, especially on pupils of the Queen Elizabeth Grammar School who shared their building with the evacuees on a 50-50 basis, local pupils occupying the classrooms only until lunch-time. For afternoon lessons, they made their way to separate buildings in town, mainly parish halls, so that the lads from the North-East could make use of the school premises in Ullswater Road.

One of the Newcastle evacuees, Peter Taylor, was to become Lord Chief Justice. Another, Brian Redhead, achieved fame as a broadcaster and commentator.

While there was a warm welcome for the Newcastle pupils from most people in Penrith, teenage boys in town were probably less enthusiastic. Romantically speaking, the Tynesiders presented glamorous rivals for the limited number of girls in the years which followed! Rivalries were inevitable, some of them quite bitter.

The Dean Road Girls' School, South Shields, was also evacuated to Penrith where the pupils enjoyed their first Christmas away from home. A South Shields newspaper wrote: "Glowing healthy faces, accounts of parties, exciting sledging, skating and sliding expeditions, stories of packed pillow-cases on Christmas morning. These are the impressions one has of the Shields bairns in Penrith."

Things did not always go so smoothly, however. The Director of Education for Westmorland, John Trevelyan, reported that of 4,700 elementary and secondary school pupils billeted in that county, 2,300 returned to their homes in Newcastle and South Shields by early-1940. Waste of public money was caused by the resultant imbalance between pupils and teachers; in one extreme case a school was reduced to 20 children but still had five teachers.

Many young men of the Territorial Army were mobilised immediately war broke out. For others, there was a slight delay, which enabled farewell services to take place. Addressing the congregation in Penrith's St Andrew's Church, the Rev. Trevor Jones said, "Brothers in the Territorial Army be sure that St Andrew's won't forget you. It will be ready for you when you come back. God be with you. We look with thankful joy upon the quiet conviction that the day will come when we will meet again." Two of the young soldiers about to leave town, John Reay and Jack Davidson, read the lessons.

The click of knitting needles was stepped up in wartime as mothers, grandmothers, sisters and girlfriends produced gloves, scarves, pullovers and other woollen comforts for their menfolk. There was a degree of rivalry at Appleby, with one band of women knitting for local men generally and a second for the exclusive use of soldiers in the 4th Battalion of the Border Regiment. Whist drives in village halls raised cash for the purchase of more wool and for 'treats' to go into parcels.

At Christmas time the men and women from Penrith who were serving in HM Forces each received a postal order for ten shillings, with a message from the town's war comforts committee which concluded: "May we add the hope that ere another Christmas dawns you will be safely back in your home town with your loved ones, whose thoughts will be specially with you at this period of the year."

Among the letters of thanks was this one from Pilot Officer George Irving: "To know that the people of one's home town do appreciate our efforts gives added incentive in reaching our aim in this grim war. Keep up the good work and keep Penrith on the map. Although our home town is small and not in the front line, it is an active cog in the huge war machine."

In June 1940 a headline in the weekly *Herald* said: "Missing, believed killed ... Penrith's first victim on active service."

James Henry Kitching, aged 19, formerly a baker in town, volunteered for the Navy on the outbreak of war. He died while working as a cook aboard a minesweeper and minelaying vessel. Information about his death was sparse but the newspaper was able to publish the message of sympathy which HM The King sent to his parents, Mr. and Mrs. William Kitching, Holme Riggs Avenue, Penrith: "The Queen and I offer our heartfelt sympathy in your great sorrow. We pray that your country's gratitude for a life so nobly given in its service may bring you some measure of consolation."

In the years which followed, there were many more reports of servicemen killed, injured and taken prisoner. For five years, the newspaper was never without at least one of these sad stories each week. Initially, there were no clear pointers as to the eventual out-

Boy Scouts contributed to the war effort of Penrith by gathering many tons of wastepaper from shops and households. Their leader, Jack Ellam, is the man standing on the ground at the back of the lorry.

come but we were sustained by an assumption that good would eventually triumph over evil. Some people still had clear memories of Britain's hard-earned victory in the Great War, old-fashioned patriotism abounded and when Winston Churchill became Prime Minister, we were reassured by his brilliant word-power. Historians have tended to belittle the great war leader but his broadcasts lifted us from the depths of depression on to a heart-warming wave of national pride and determination.

Human tragedies were not confined to the death of loved ones in battle. Magistrates at Appleby were told the sad story of a woman who had given false information when registering the birth of her female child, in 1943. She entered the name of her husband as the girl's father but the registrar found that he was a soldier and had been a prisoner of war in Germany since 1940. The woman had moved away from her home town for the birth of the child, which was then adopted. Her love affair with another man, during her husband's enforced absence, would have remained a secret but for the registrar's uncovering of the subterfuge. The court fine of £5 was probably not the outcome she regretted most. Other brief wartime romances led to a big increase in venereal diseases. The Cumberland Infirmary, Carlisle, ran special clinics on three afternoons a week.

The aspects of war of which people in small Cumbrian towns were most directly aware were the black-out and the rationing of food, fuel and clothing. Not a glimmer of light was permitted, for Hitler's bombers might be flying overhead. The black-out caused dark and depressing streets, especially in the depths of winter. Occasionally, patrolling policemen spotted a chink of light or an electric light bulb glowing in an uncurtained room. On-the-spot warnings sufficed in some cases but many householders were summoned to appear in the police courts. Fines were generally £1 or £1 10s. (£1.50), although the figure was reduced to ten shillings if only a flickering candle was spotted by a passing PC.

There were wry chuckles when the normal procedure was reversed. A member of the Penrith public reported an offence by the constabulary – a light bulb shining in the courtroom at the police station, with the black-out curtain not in position. The senior officer on duty, Inspector John Stanley Nelson, did not follow the example of a distinguished namesake by turning a blind eye. He took the blame for the lapse and was fined £1 10s. (£1.50) in the courtroom where the offence was committed. "We must act without fear or favour," said the presiding magistrate, Richard McVittie.

How could love be to blame for a breach of the black-out regulations? Well, claimed a Penrith householder, a maidservant was writing a letter to a boyfriend, serving in the Army, and "was lost in love and oblivious to the offence she was committing by allowing her black-out blind to flap".

Motorists were required to use minimal lighting. The first person to go before a local court for a breach of these rules was a man from Newby, in North Westmorland. JPs at Hackthorpe fined him £1 because the lights on his car were not screened effectively.

Cumbrian countryfolk tend to have healthy appetites. The introduction of wartime rationing made it inevitable that there would be determined efforts to evade the restrictions and the black market flourished, especially in close-knit rural communities. A Penrith insuranceman made regular calls at a Skelton village farm for supplies of butter. As he left on one occasion, with the vital packet hidden in the back of the car, a local policeman dismounted from his pushbike and signalled him to stop.

"Have you been to that farm for butter?" the bobby inquired solemnly.

Rather hesitantly, the insuranceman replied, "As a matter of fact, I have."

"Good, isn't it?" said the guardian of the law. "I get mine there as well."

The Ministry of Food published advertisements explaining that rationing was essential because it prevented the wastage of food, divided supplies evenly, prevented uncertainty and boosted the war effort (by freeing ships to bring in armaments and other vital imports). Bacon, ham, sugar and butter were among the first foodstuffs to be rationed. Meat came next, in March 1940, when it was announced that adults would be restricted to 1s 10d. (9p) worth a week and children to 11d. (4½ p) worth, although at that stage ration coupons were not needed to buy liver, tripe, kidney or for poultry and game. To help householders to cope with limited amounts, there were demonstrations on food economy, some of them at Electricity House, Penrith.

The rationing of tea, later in 1940, caused a furore at the annual meeting of the Federation of Westmorland Women's Institutes. The Burneside delegate put forward a recommendation that the customary tea breaks at WI meetings should be given up for the duration of the war, "in the interests of economy and to set an example".

A WI meeting without a cuppa! Surely not. The tea break was the most enjoyable part of the evening. Without refreshment, members would be in a state of fatigue by the end of the evening. The idea was firmly rejected.

One of the earliest breaches of rationing came to light because a Penrith doctor's letters to his mother, in Southern Ireland, were checked by a postal censor. He spotted a tell-tale passage: "The bacon you sent is delicious. I really do appreciate the first-class butter and bacon you send."

The Ministry of Food viewed such cases so seriously that fines of £100 could be imposed. Penrith magistrates decided that a £1 penalty would suffice, as it was the first prosecution of its kind to go before the court.

N. Arnison and Sons, of The House of Fashion, Penrith, invited women to visit the dress material department to select "a lovely Viyella thirty-six design" and the paper pattern they preferred. A dress would then be cut with perfect sureness of line, customers were assured.

But the fashion parade was restricted severely by the introduction of the Clothes Rationing Order in 1941. Each person was allocated 66 coupons a year, which did not go far. The *Herald* quoted the case of a young woman who used all but two of her coupons at one go, as she fitted herself out for a new job on a farm near Penrith. In this list of her purchases the numbers of clothing points are in brackets: Three black hose (6), two nightdresses (6), three overalls (9), three pairs of knickers (9), three cotton dresses (21), two ounces of wool (1), one pair of corsets (3), and three working aprons (9).

Sales of silk stockings and luxurious lingerie suffered. Durability became the watchword when buying clothes; style and novelty had to go by the board. Tough 'utility' stockings were better value than the silken variety. The Board of Trade ruled that men's socks must be shortened by five inches – and this in September 1942, just before the onset of wintry weather. A writer in the *Herald* commented: "The pre-war sock was never remarkable for its length but the new style will hardly take it halfway to the suspender."

Even cleanliness was rationed. Announcing that soap could only by bought if people had coupons, the Ministry of Food stated in February 1942: "The oils and soaps used in soap manufacture occupy much shipping space and some of this must be saved for food."

Later that year came the blitz of the bulls' eyes, as sweets and chocolates were rationed – a quarter of a pound a week - although merely having sweet coupons was not a guarantee that you could get the sweets. Supplies ran short and children with sweet teeth cycled from shop to shop, hoping to find one where counters had been replenished. A labourer preferred beer to sweets or chocolate, and offered to sell his sweet coupons in a Penrith pub, the General Wolfe. Unfortunately for him, he made the offer to an off-duty police officer who promptly "booked" him for the offence. The magistrates took a dim view and the labourer's beer money was £5 lighter after he appeared in court.

Among other sacrifices which had to be made, by direction of the Ministry of Food in 1942, was the ending of the production of ice-cream. Ministry men said that the manufacture and sale of the delicacy represented much manpower, transport, raw materials and packing, in all of which the country must economise.

We were even told to limit the depth of the bathwater, with a view to keeping down heating costs. Five inches of water were enough for the ablutions, the nation was told. The King was said to have set an example and the top London hotels followed his lead, some drawing thin red lines round the baths as a guide.

People were constantly urged to be canny, not only in the use of food and fuel, but also in preserving goods which could be put to an alternative uses. There were salvage drives for bones (which could be used in explosives), metal (for bombs), rags (for blankets), paper (for shell containers), rubber (for dinghies) and string (for naval charts).

The keyword was "Save" – and this applied not only to bones, paper and metal but to hard cash! To boost war savings, by purchases of stamps and certificates, annual drives were held in towns and country areas, with titles like 'Warship week', 'Wings for Victory week' and 'Salute the Soldier week'. They were launched in some style, with the reading of telegrams of support from the Chancellor of the Exchequer, bands playing and an Army colonel taking the salute at marchpasts of Home Guardsmen, ARP wardens, Army and ATC cadets, Land Army girls, WVS, and even the youngsters of the Brownies, Girl Guides and Boy Scouts. Towns and villages set targets and invariably exceeded them; the hamlet of Newbiggin (Temple Sowerby), with only 110 people, was among the most ambitious with a target of £2,000. Opening ceremonies of town efforts provided opportunities for shows of patriotism and the strength of the voluntary units.

The 'prince' of war savings supporters was Jonathan Fisher, a man in his twenties, of Ivegill, Carlisle, who, despite blindness, collected vast sums, walking from house to house, initially with the aid of his sheep dog, 'Don', which later died. He received a telegram from the Treasury which concluded: "The £5,540 which you have collected, despite many disabilities, including the loss of your dog, is a wonderful total, and Sir Kingsley Wood is very grateful to you."

Quite apart from money invested in war savings certificates, the people of Westmorland gave generously to a fund to buy their own Spitfire fighter aircraft. Authoress Nancy Price initiated the idea, an influential committee was formed and there was a swift and spirited response, ranging from a shilling from a six-year-old evacuee to the £250 given by a Windermere man. The Rev. C. F. Cardale, vicar of Kirkby Stephen, formed a football team whose matches brought in cash, and Women's Institutes, Home Guard units and village collectors all rallied to the cause. Inside eight weeks, over £8,000 was raised – enough for a Spitfire and a half! Lord Beaverbrook, as Minister for Aircraft Production, promised the people of the county that the Spitfire would be named "Westmorland" and would win them "glory in the skies" in defence of their liberty.

Long after the war of 1939-45, any mention of the Home Guard seems to cause people to chuckle at the likeable characters of the BBC Television comedy series, "Dad's Army" – pompous, garrulous, bloody-minded, undeniably loyal. In reality, of course, the amateur soldiers were much more responsible and better organised than Captain Mainwaring and his men of TV fame.

It was in May 1940 that the War Minister, Anthony Eden, announced the formation of the Local Defence Volunteers (as the Home Guardsmen were originally known). Within a few minutes the first Cumbrian volunteers were arriving at police stations to "sign up" and inside a couple of days the response throughout Cumberland and Westmorland was 3,100, including 397 at Penrith and 237 at Appleby. Enemy parachutists were "assured of a warm reception", said a report in the *Herald*.

It was a fraught time. With the British Expeditionary Force retreating across France in the face of a determined German onslaught, a chill ran across the nation, as war seemed to draw closer, even to Cumbria's remote hills and dales. The response to the call for a Home Guard reflected the spirit of the nation and served as a morale-booster at a time of poignant anxiety for the future of mankind.

4

Fair sex in farming

Imagine a girl typist tackling a tractor. Or a mannequin manipulating a milking machine. Or a hairdresser cutting hay.

However unlikely the prospect, twelve young women, aged between 16 and 28, arrived for training in agriculture at Newton Rigg Farm School, near Penrith, in October, 1939, pioneers of the Women's Land Army. In their natty uniforms, they brought a tinge of glamour to the meadows, byres, poultry houses and farmyards and, in many cases, proved that girls of town and city could play a useful role in agriculture and settle down in the countryside, far away from busy streets and cinemas and without the guarantee of an eight-hour day.

Although turning out at 6 o'clock in the morning, they still found time to apply a smear of lipstick and a puff of face powder. In the beginning they had some trouble in telling a duck from a drake, but they were eager to learn. They were soon digging in manure, milking cows, feeding the hens and doing other routine but demanding jobs.

As the war years passed, the workforce on Cumbrian farms was gradually boosted by the influx of enemy prisoners, both German and Italian. The general view was that the Teutonic thoroughness of the Germans made them first-rate workers. The Italians (or "Eyeties") were not held in such high regard, although they apparently had other characteristics which appealed to some of the women living near the camps, many casual relationships resulting.

Farmers needed the help, for most of them had a hectic war. In collaboration with the newly-formed war agricultural executive committees, and with the inducement of special subsidies, they worked hard to produce vital crops, initially potatoes. The humble tatie achieved stardom in wartime, a vital part of the British diet.

"Eat more potatoes instead," urged the Ministry of Food adverts in newspapers. "Remember that every time you eat potatoes instead of bread, you release food ships for vital war work."

The message was repeated week after week, month after month. A potato plan was recommended. Housewives should dish up potatoes in ways other than plain boiled, serve them for breakfast on three days a week, and refuse "seconds" of other foods, filling up the family with even more taties.

A patriotic rhyme of the time, published in the adverts, went like this:

> If you have a luncheon date,
> And there's bread beside your plate,
> Give that bread back to the waiter,
> Fill yourself up with pertater.

However hungry they might be, families were bound to become weary of boiled potatoes, so the imaginative men of the Ministry recommended them in different guises: Potato Jane (sliced potato and cheese, baked), Potato Mousaka (potatoes, cheese, carrots, dried egg, baked) and Cornish pasties with potato pastry.

While the emphasis was on the excellence of the tatie as a wartime filler, the limelight of Ministry of Food publicity also fell on other root crops, such as the swede turnip which was said to be as rich in Vitamin C as oranges and lemons. Reduced to a pulp, the humble swede masqueraded as an ingredient of marmalade or strawberry jam!

Or why not a carrot sandwich? "Add two parts of grated raw carrot to one part of finely-shredded white heart of cabbage and bind together with chutney or sweet pickle. Pepper and salt to taste. Filling tastes best in wholemeal bread." The savoury-tasting carrot pancake was another possibility. It developed a deliciously crisp crust when pan-fried in a little fat, the Ministry of Food advised.

With potatoes such an essential food, the "war ag" committees made orders as to the extra acreages to be ploughed on individual farms. Failure to comply could lead to hefty fines – £20, with costs, in the case of one elderly Cumbrian farmer accused of "wilful defiance", despite a plea that he had insufficient manpower, with only his wife and a 23-year-old woman to assist him.

Most farmers responded to the call to plough more land. A unique event in the village hall at Lazonby, in April 1940, recognised the ploughmen's endeavours. Three hundred of them were guests of honour at a free supper and concert. One of the toasts was to "Men of the land".

Lazonby, in the fertile Eden Valley, was at the very heart of a district where, over a few months, the colour of the landscape changed from green to brown. The area made a massive contribution to the 35,000 acres of Cumberland land ploughed up during the spring. Imprinted on the hall wall, as the farm men enjoyed their free feed, were the words, "God speed the plough".

Broadcaster Wilfred Pickles visited Cumberland and gave a radio talk on his impressions of the farming scene. He said: "Only one thing has changed and that is the face of the land itself. All over England more crops have had to be grown to feed both man and beast. The story of ploughed up grassland means very little to a town chap like myself when given in so many figures – but when you go to Cumberland and see some of the steep slopes on the fellside ploughed up, then you realise what 'plough up' means. Land which has never known the plough is growing foodstuffs, which will lighten the terrible strain on our seamen."

But the farmer in wartime was both hero and villain. He was suspected of the excessive slaughter of pigs, of black market deals in butter and eggs and of misusing his allocation of petrol. Checks on cars outside cinemas and dance halls, and even at country churches where funerals were taking place, led to farmers being fined for the wrongful use of petrol. If they wanted to pay a last tribute to the dead, they should travel to church by pushbike or on foot.

Whatever the Ministry of Food might advocate, people in country areas fancied something a bit more tasty, which led to a spate of cases of the killing of pigs without having proper licences. So desperate were some folk for a breakfast of bacon and egg or a tasty supper of sausage, black pudding and chips, that porkers were killed in the most unlikely of places – including a pub garage at dead of night – and without proper authorisation. Ministry investigators were alerted, sometimes because customers were too talkative about the sausage they had enjoyed, and fines of up to £10 were imposed on the offending pig-rearers when they appeared in Cumbrian police courts.

Other dilemmas facing farmers could land them in trouble. The military mind did not comprehend the problems of agriculture and insisted that farmers and farm workers should join the Home Guard. With heavier crops to produce, many of them claimed that they could not afford the time to attend parades and training sessions – and found themselves before the courts on charges of "being absent without reasonable excuse". A Langwathby farmer pleaded that the demands of cows calving, plus added production levels, made it impossible for him to attend Home Guard duties, even though the parade ground was only 100 yards from the farm. His words did not impress the magistrates at Penrith who saw the non-attendance as "wilful disobedience" and fined the farmer £7 10s (£7.50).

JPs at Appleby were more sympathetic and understanding and dismissed the charges against eight men, farmers and farm workers, who claimed that they had "reasonable excuses" for not attending Home Guard duties, including the wildness of the weather, the fact that a thresher had to be repaired, a bout of illness and the rescuing of lambs from floods. "One has great sympathy with the men on farms in their self-sacrificing efforts to make the best of both worlds," said an editorial in the *Herald*, referring to the conflicting demands on farmers by the war agricultural executive committee and the military authorities.

Although a senior officer once agreed that in the early days of war, members of the Home Guard "were little better than glorified Boy Scouts", the improvement was impressive and creditable. What was originally a gallant band of ill-trained, ill-armed, ill-equipped enthusiasts developed into a well-trained, adequately armed and fully equipped army – the recognised first line of defence against an invasion from the sea. As many Home Guardsmen had served in the 1914-18 war, their leadership was generally sound and zealous.

The 10th Westmorland (Appleby) Battalion so impressed in a big exercise that the *Herald* reporter was inspired to write: "Romans, Normans and others have learnt, to their distress, the natural strength of this rugged country, for defences and forts, long since disintegrated, bear testimony to the fact that an eye for country is no modern acquisition. And now, with all the ancient tradition in nearly every family resident along the fell, the Briton of today stands waiting for the Hun barbarian."

Two farmers, on a visit to Penrith auction mart, were unable to produce their identity cards when asked for them by a policeman. "It is a pity you do not have something better to do," they told the officer. Magistrates reproached them for their insolent words, as well as fining them £1 apiece for not producing the cards.

Increased food production on the farm was not the only usage of land which boosted the war effort. Most people in Penrith and the surrounding countryside became aware that soldiers were encamped in Lowther Park, close to the battlemented castle of the Lowther family, and at Warcop, in the Upper Eden Valley. The local newspapers were prevented from reporting such activities by war-time censorship, but more astute readers must have spotted clues on the public notices page. A grand dance in the village institute at Askham on Easter Monday of 1942 was advertised as costing 1s 6d (7½p) per person but for HM Forces the price was only a shilling (5p). Penrith YMCA football club held a dance in St Andrew's parish hall, for which the music was supplied by "The new RTR dance band". RTR stood for Royal Tank Regiment.

The veil of secrecy had lifted slightly by June 1942 when a sports meeting, cricket match and variety show were staged by the Penrith troops entertainment committee. The list of sports results in the newspaper referred to units like the RTR and Traffic Control but there were no precise references as to where the soldiers were based. The events "catered for the off-duty hours of military units that happened to be located in the district".

Penrith people knew full well that something special was being done at Lowther because each evening they looked from their windows to see blinding lights illuminating the night sky to the south of the town. These remained a mystery for months until word finally got out that a secret weapon was under trial.

The Canal Defence Light (better known as CDL) was developed by the British Army with the intention of blinding the enemy. From a projector on a specially adapted tank, a fan-shaped beam of light lit up the area of attack and dazzled the enemy. While the attacker enjoyed all the benefits of moving forward in artificial light, the opposition forces could see nothing, as the advancing tanks and infantry were concealed behind the powerful CDLs. The device had been considered for some years but the outbreak of war gave impetus to the idea and a CDL school was set up at Lowther Castle, the officers and men concerned originally living under canvas in a sea of mud, before occupying parts of the castle.

Field Marshal Earl Alexander's intention was to use CDLs in the second battle of El Alamein but they were not ready at that juncture and it was decided that the debut should be reserved for later European operations. In fact, the novel weapon was never used at all and, in the ensuing inquests, this has been seen as military short-sightedness. Some 6,000 officers and men attended the CDL school and a total of 1,850 tanks were converted to the CDL role but we will never know how they would have fared in the heat of battle. They only served a secondary purpose in providing illumination for the crossing of the Rhine.

As the war years passed and the secrecy melted away, the presence of CDL and the Royal Tank Regiment at Lowther became widely known. A team from the school played in a Carlisle football league under the title of CDL and the matches were reported by the newspapers. When the unit left Lowther, the Penrith town club took over fixtures from CDL until the soccer season ended.

Locations in the Eden Valley figured in other notable contributions to the war effort of 1939-45 but not until peace returned were the details revealed. While the world waited for the Allied forces to invade Europe in 1944, some 4,000 acres of land near the pretty village of Warcop, in Upper Eden, represented the battlefront for men preparing for the big assault. The men of the Royal Armoured Corps replaced farmers and shepherds in this pleasant corner of the countryside, and the rumble of tanks and the chatter of their guns became familiar sounds.

It all began long before that memorable day in June 1944 when the Allied might crossed the English Channel, to be unleashed against the enemy. Land-breakers and road-makers blazed a trail by creating roads over the lower slopes of the fells between Brough and Appleby, observation towers were built and targets sprang up. Huts grew like mushrooms, soon to be occupied by men in khaki battle-dress and jaunty black berets.

Once the tanks and armoured cars arrived, with guns jutting aggressively, the firing started. Day after day, month after month, it continued, all with the aim of perfecting the fighting skills of the tank crews. RAC men by the thousand arrived and departed. Many of the armoured units trained near Warcop were later to the forefront in the Normandy landings. This, then, is the proud history of the Warcop range, a history which continued in peacetime and still continues – a familiar sight to all who travel along the busy east-west route, the A66.

Warcop lives on as an Army establishment but long forgotten is the part played by another picturesque area where battle scenes were enacted, near lovely Martindale on the east side of Ullswater. About 200 men at a time became battle-hardened as they set out on patrol with their faces smeared with camouflage cream and wearing steel helmets with coverings of foliage. Exercises became known as "battle innoculation" by bringing trainees under fire to accustom them to the sounds of war. Assault boats were launched on Ullswater while other exercises included sleeping out on the Lakeland fells through the night, with bivouacs made out of groundsheets. Bren gunners' tracer bullets made spectacular displays, as they ricocheted high in the air.

In October 1946 the War Office included lands at Martindale and Warcop among their long-term requirements for training. Few people opposed the plans for Warcop but there was steely resistance to the further use of land at Martindale from North Westmorland Rural Council, the Friends of the Lake District, the Council for the Preservation of Rural England and the National Trust.

Thousands of people who annually relish the scenic glory of Ullswater from its pleasure boats, the *Lady of the Lake* and the *Raven*, do not realise that the vessels had a wartime role in the training of young sailors. A sea school was evacuated to Ravencragg, a big house at Howtown, by the side of the lake, and the teenage pupils had their first experience of steering and berthing under the guidance of a steamer captain named Band.

On a farm at Whinfell, a few miles east of Penrith, a small airfield was set up as an out-of-the-way base for aeroplanes of several types, all masked by camouflage nets. Despite the attempts to obscure the aircraft, they were spotted by the Germans, whose sneering propagandist, Lord Haw Haw, mentioned the fact in one of his regular broadcasts, aimed at destroying British morale. The wartime contribution of the town of Alston, high in the Pennines, was widely unknown, and unsung, until many months after peace returned.

There was a desperate shortage of mortar bomb cases in 1940 and a foundry was needed to produce them. At a time when a German invasion was considered a possibility, Alston was suggested because it was well inland and, also, because an old stocking factory, in the process of being demolished, was thought to be suitable as a nucleus for a foundry. The work of conversion was carried out in the black-out gloom of the long winter nights of 1940-41, often by the flickering light of stable lanterns and candles in bottles. The major problem was to find a local workforce to operate the furnaces when the available labour consisted mainly of shepherds and farmers. An old man of 73 was drawn out of retirement – one of only two workers who had been in a steel foundry before.

Despite the staffing problems, the demand for bomb cases was satisfied. Chains and castings were produced for the Admiralty and, before the end of hostilities, the foundry workers played a part in the building of Mulberry Dock. The shortages of wartime were many and varied. One of them led to a Government decision, in mid-1942, to remove railings and metal gates to provide a boost of materials for the armaments industry.

What could Penrith's railings provide after they were pitched into the melting pot? A newspaper reporter, covering the story, asked the question and then provided the answer: 110 submarine torpedoes, or twenty 6-inch naval guns, or eight capstans for cruisers, or two naval 15-inch guns, or eight cruiser tanks, or 780 anti-aircraft shells.

The "rape of the railings" caused a lot of discontent. Even urban councillors were unhappy about the demolition of the barricades around public property and made a special plea for the retention of the Castle Park gateway, which formed a part of Penrith's memorial to those who died in the 1914-18 war. Had the iron gates been purloined, it would have been an act not only of vandalism but sacrilege.

With the war over, there was an international "invasion" of parts of east Cumbria. Former Army camps on the fringes of Penrith, at Carleton and Brougham, housed "displaced persons" – Latvians, Estonians, Czechs and Ukrainians who had been made homeless and were trying to make a fresh start. Other Latvians – about 150 of them who had volunteered to do agricultural work in this country – found accommodation in the former prisoner of war camp at Merrythought, near Calthwaite, from where they were taken to work on lorries each morning.

By far the biggest transformation saw the former Army camp of brick-built and Nissen-type huts in Lowther Park converted into what was virtually a new village to accommodate 600 people from Poland. They had their own school, church and community centre and their football team, Lowther Polonia, played in the local leagues. In the fullness of time many of the refugees, who found sanctuary in and near Penrith in the 1940s, integrated into the Cumbrian community.

5

Lost Tuesdays

"Noo than, Joe. Hoos thi fettle? Let's hev thi bit crack."

"Hesta sin oor Billy lately? Must bi mair than a twelve month sin wi' met up. Ah nivver set eyes on 'im, save fer a funeral or a weddin'."

The voices which rang out in the shopping streets of Penrith were richly laced with local dialect. In the far-off days of the 1940s and 1950s it seemed everybody knew almost everybody else, their jobs, who they married or courted, their interests, their ailments, their mutual acquaintances. A walk along Devonshire Street or Middlegate was punctuated with stoppages to greet or chat, inquire about mutual friends or share a joke.

Like other Cumbrian market towns, Penrith remains friendly and vibrant enough but, perhaps, we don't greet each other with quite the same enthusiasm and, with "offcomers" about, the use of dialect is restricted, and voices are more subdued. Perhaps, the biggest change is that Tuesdays in Penrith aren't what they used to be. All towns change gently, imperceptibly, but the character – and the characters – of our old-time Tuesdays are no more.

The root cause was the move out of town of the auction mart; the subsequent building of a Safeway supermarket on part of the mart site was another major factor. I remember Tuesday when it was not only market day but a day of shapely women in tweed suits and sensible hats, chattering amiably – concerned females, with baskets brimful, who made the most of the once-a-week opportunity to socialise. Towards mid-afternoon, with most of the shopping gathered in, conversational crowds of them assembled on street corners and outside cafes, waiting for an old friend before going inside for a cup of tea and a cake. They valued the "crack" more than the snack.

In the busy town centre the groups presented a weekly hindrance to pedestrians but nobody complained, for the very presence of the women represented prosperity. While the buxom pavement chatterers were in prolonged and animated discussion, their menfolk enjoyed a different kind of conviviality. After an hour or two at the auction mart, at the top of Castlegate, they wanted refreshments and many drifted away towards handy pubs – the Agricultural (or "Agri"), next door to the mart, or the Railway Tavern, the Station or the Museum. In the depths of winter, the first request as they entered the bar might well be: "Gis a hot toddy, will ta"

Over foaming pints, bottles of beer, Guinness, Mackeson or "a laal drop o'short", mart prices were debated – and frequently deplored – but before long the dominoes were clicking and the darts thudding, as they settled in for a session of some duration. Licensing hours were extended on Tuesdays to cope with the demand. Later, as they left the pubs, the farmers' next call was often Tommy Dayson's milkbar, at the foot of Castlegate, for a steadying cup of coffee and a couple of generous ham sandwiches.

Tuesdays were days apart from the rest of the week. The streets and squares were livelier and chummier and first-name greetings rang out: "Hellow Sam. Hoos this weather soot th'?" The women, still deep in conversation, looked out for the return of their men, some rather wobbly after too much ale.

"Let's just slip inta t' Gloucester for another" ... "Nea, Ah think Ah should be gitten yam, Ah've hed a skinful a'riddy" ... "Divent worry, Mary'll wait for th'. She'll hev gone for a cuppatea and a fancy keake" ... "Cu thisel on then, but just yan."

The older order changeth. With the auction mart now sited a mile from town, the Tuesday throng has fallen away. Faster motoring enables shoppers to travel from rural remoteness to seek bargains in faraway cities, in shops more opulent than they could hope to find in a country town.

Another market day memory is of cattle and sheep being driven through the streets, on their way to rural farms or to be loaded aboard trains at a railway siding. Just occasionally something went

The last of the Penrith street traders — Harold Hardisty, who sold fruit and vegetables from a pitch in Middlegate. *(Alec Fraser)*

wrong. The drovers lost control and an errant bullock entered a town centre house through an open door or caused chaos in the environs of St Andrew's Church, sending shoppers scuttling for safety.

Not for many years has the town seen the likes of Bob Armer and the other old-time bullock wallopers, aided and abetted by farm dogs, as they steered lumbering herds through crowded streets or past children as they made their way home from school. Auction mart activity is remote from the town and the clutter and atmosphere of market day have never been experienced by the younger generation of today.

Penrith throbbed with activity every Tuesday. Farm supply men displayed their wares in Corn Market; a potential customer might be invited for a sup of coffee in Dayson's milkbar or something rather stronger in the Gloucester Arms, both within about 100 yards or so of the suppliers' stands. Hopefully, deals would be struck for farm equipment or a load of cattle feed.

The outdoor market filled Great Dockray with stalls and shoppers. Eager housewives looked for bargains among the carpets, kitchen utensils, bedding, clothing or the fish and fruit stalls. A few traders offered their wares alongside streets nearer to the town centre – from the pavement in Middlegate or from trestle tables set up in Devonshire Street. Among the last of the street traders were Harold Hardisty and Edwin Lee, the latter a true character whose genial patter boosted the sale of fruit and veg. from his Great Dockray stall on Saturdays.

Another personality of the 1950s was Tommy Borrowdale, a handicapped man who sold evening newspapers from a battered pram positioned beside the Musgrave Monument clock, in the middle of town. Business was best on Saturday nights as football supporters bought papers to read accounts of the performances of Carlisle United and Penrith, or to check their football coupons.

There is no longer the same inclination to stop and stare that once there was – no longer groups of middle-aged men idling their time away on one side of the town centre, or rather older types who spent hours on the broader pavement opposite, on wooden seats. The loungers seemed to be drawn, magnet-like, by the Musgrave Monument, a clock tower at the junction of the three main shopping streets. Retired veterans, men without work and various others simply stopped to enjoy the chatter or to watch the world pass by. For there was more to see of the outside world in those pre-motorway days when north-south traffic surged through the middle of town, and massive vehicles had to queue before negotiating narrow sections of the road, sometimes with needle-threading precision.

Among the cheerful old men on the bench-type seats was Ernie Burrell, a local sporting star of an earlier era, who occasionally called across passers-by, proffered a bulging paper bag and inquired, "What d'ya think o' them?" The bag was full of mushrooms, their undersides still pinkish to show that it was not long since they had been picked. "How aboot them for tea?" inquired Ernie. He was proud of the fact that he knew where the best mushrooms grew but would not disclose his secrets.

There were other popular meeting places. Long before the days of unisex salons, with attractive young women to wash and cut, all-male hairdressing shops were scenes of lively chatter and, sometimes, fierce argument. In Jack Pounder's establishment in Penrith's Little Dockray, the occupants of the three chairs debated controversies, both local and national, with those seated behind them, waiting for a haircut or a shave. Jack not only presided, but made his own forceful contributions and quips while removing whiskers with his cut-throat style razor. It was good entertainment – and good for business. Local government often loomed large, especially if there was a councillor in one of the chairs or the local rate had just been increased. If the conversation turned to football, as often it did, the fortunes of "Jack's team", the men of Burnley FC, were generally highlighted.

The cat which slept in the sunshine on a shop doorstep in King Street, Penrith, was an unlikely sales promoter for Charlie Dixon, a

dispensing chemist. Thomas the cat was very popular with children who loved to fondle his fur and urged their mothers to patronise the shop. "Let's go to see Thomas," they pleaded, although their mothers often had no real reason for entering the premises.

The chemist's shop of the 1950s was unorthodox because mixed among the potions and lotions, toothpastes and lipsticks, on the counter, were tomatoes from Charlie Dixon's greenhouse and honey from his hives. Charlie, whose joviality masked an astuteness in

In the 1950s, there was the reward of petting Thomas, the shop cat of chemist, Charlie Dixon – an unintentional form of sales gimmickry!

business, was an entertaining conversationalist and loved a friendly argument on a topic of the day. He caused a furore in town with a move to place a vending machine, for the sale of condoms, outside the shop; way back in the 1950s do-gooders in the community were alarmed by the prospect, although there were many others who would have welcomed a less embarrassing way of making purchases.

Buying condoms – then under another name, by the way – called for a degree of shameless bravado, for the little packets were never on display and approaches to chemists' assistants were reduced to self-conscious whispers. Single men who made such purchases sometimes had the distinct feeling that their activities were frowned upon, while their girlfriends were seen as forward hussies.

Inevitably, town centre premises have seen many changes. You could get the impression that the era of the Cumberland sausage, Sunday roast and tatie pot is ebbing away, and that Cumbrians must now have a remarkable appetite for exotic food, so numerous are the restaurants and takeaways which specialise in foreign fare; Chinese, Indian and Italian dishes all compete with traditional meals.

One Italian restaurant, established in 1994, is in the building in St Andrew's Churchyard which once pulsated with the production of a weekly newspaper, the now-defunct *Penrith Observer*. The chink of wineglasses, the throb of Latin music, and the ordering of spaghetti, lasagnes and other delicacies contrast sharply with bygone days when the place echoed to the hammering of typewriters, the clunk of Linotype machines and the pounding of the press as the *Observer* was printed, for sale every Tuesday.

Penrith has plenty of public houses, although some of the characterful old hostelries have now heard the calling of "Time, gentlemen, please" for the last time. The Fish, along with other premises at the foot of Castlegate, was demolished to make room for the Poet's Walk shopping mall. The Duke's Head, in Angel Lane, was later converted into a unisex hairdressing salon. The Old Crown, in King Street, was turned into an office block. Two other King Street hostelries also disappeared, the Horse and Farrier becoming flats and the Mitre housing a firm of solicitors. The night of the closure of the White Horse, in Friargate, was attended by local cricketers, a gesture which recognised the fact that the pub was the birthplace of Penrith cricket club over a century before.

There was an earthiness about many of the old-style public houses. They catered for men who, in the 1950s, chewed black twist tobacco, so that a spittoon containing sawdust was essential to the bar equipment.

The heart of Penrith is marked by the Musgrave Monument clock tower, built in 1861. This picture recalls the street scene before the traffic enhancement scheme of 1999, making Devonshire Street, in the foreground, a one-way street. Stone setts now make up the road surface. (*Frederick C. Wilson*)

Womenfolk were not encouraged unless in the company of their husbands and, even then, they were expected to sit and drink in the smoke room, rather than in the bar where the hard drinkers congregated and cursed their luck as they threw darts or played dominoes. In any case, few pubs had toilets for females. If women customers were known to the publican and his wife, they generally had permission to use the household's lavatory.

Middle-aged and elderly men patronised the same pubs, year after year, becoming almost part of the family. Their thirst for mild and bitter beer was vital to the wellbeing of the host and hostess. Few inns sold food, apart from nuts and potato crisps. An exception to this rule occurred just before Easter each year when, according to long tradition, each customer received a dish of carlings, tasty black peas flavoured with butter and scraps of ham.

Penrith's favourite tipple was Glasson's beer, brewed and bottled in the town for more than a century before the company was taken over by a Blackburn company in 1959. The licensed houses of Glassons could be identified by their distinctive inn signs, all the

Victory parade — Shortly after winning the Grand National at Aintree in 1978, the racehorse, "Lucius", was walked through the streets of Penrith for an official reception at the Town Hall. "Lucius" was trained by Gordon Richards at his Greystoke stables. Behind on bikes are jockeys Bob Davies, Jonjo O'Neill, David Goulding and Ron Barry. (*Frederick C. Wilson*)

work of David Creighton, a local painter and decorator whose skills extended to imaginative painting. Signs which marked houses like the Dog and Gun at Skelton, the Shepherd's at Langwathby, and the White Horse in Penrith, among many others, were painted individually and took about a week apiece. David was paid £5 each at a time when the pound in your pocket was of real value.

Reflective of the one-time booziness of Penrith, the town has had more than a hundred pubs over the past 250 years, although most of them served their last pints long ago. Occasionally, the pubs catered for a couple of holidaymakers or a commercial traveller. In the days of the two or three-day sales of pedigree Shorthorn cattle there was a demand for beds from farmers and dealers and, in some cases, children were moved out to sleep elsewhere, so that the pubs could capitalise fully on the added business. As the visitors became "residents" for two or three nights, they could be served with drink far beyond the normal closing time of ten o'clock.

One of the landlord's last tasks before going to bed was to leave under a bucket, placed alongside the back door, a bottle of beer, a bottle opener and a glass. Policemen, checking the premises in the early hours of the morning, appreciated a drink before moving on!

Fewer policemen patrol the shopping streets, compared with the 1950s and 60s. Generally more remote than in days long past, they keep an eye on the town centre by means of strategically-sited overhead cameras, just as shops and supermarkets try to deter any light-fingered customers.

The movement of the auction mart was a major happening in itself. Even more far-reaching was the fact that the old mart site was sold to Safeway, the supermarket chain, for this switched the focus of the shoppers away from the town centre. Councillors initially opposed the trend for building society offices and travel agencies to replace shops in the main streets, but it soon became clear that there was little alternative if they wanted to avoid untidy gaps and empty properties in the street scene.

Even as these words are written, experts in technology predict that within 10 years traditional high streets will be ousted by "shopless shopping". Instead of walking into town, pondering outside colourful shop windows and chatting with shop assistants, we will rely on Internet and E-mail when seeking bargain buys. Perish the thought!

6

Birth of a bank

A wet and windy night on the farms in east Cumbria was the prelude to a unique bit of banking history. On sheep farms in the 1960s all ewes gave birth to their lambs outside, in the fields, whereas nowadays many are housed in modern sheep sheds, some of them fitted with closed-circuit television cameras, enabling farmers to monitor progress from the warmth of their bedrooms.

The wild overnight weather, all those years ago, caused a spate of losses. Some of the ewes, having given birth to large single lambs, were so exhausted that they were unable to lick them to stimulate circulation and the offspring were lost. Other new mothers walked about with two or three little lambs, too many for one ewe to feed. Shepherds try to give every ewe a lamb to nurture by splitting up triplets, or even pairs, but it is vital that this is done quickly to avoid the rejection of foster lambs.

Matthew Savage, a jovial man who farmed at Aikbank, Calthwaite, was making his customary market day visit to Penrith by car when the spotted John Gibson, of Castlesteads Farm, Plumpton, waiting for the Ribble bus. Good neighbour that he was, 'Mattha' gave John a lift into town and, on the way, their conversation turned to the morning's lambing. John was short of a foster lamb and Matthew had one to spare, so it was agreed that John should collect the orphan for a small cash consideration.

Later that day, the two had lunch at the Lakeland Cafe, near the auction mart, with Jim Kitching, the secretary of Penrith branch of the National Farmers' Union. It was a significant get-together because, after hearing of the lamb transaction, Jim Kitching sug-

Prize rams of the Swaledale breed draw big crowds to Kirkby Stephen auction mart every autumn. (*Frederick C. Wilson*)

gested that, as NFU secretary, he was in the ideal position to keep a register of spare lambs; farmers could telephone him if they had a surplus or if they required an additional lamb. The 'lamb bank' was born, with a self-appointed bank manager.

Jim Kitching and his staff manned the 'phones in the early days but the 'bank' was later taken over by BBC Radio Cumbria, who broadcast the needs of flockmasters two or three times a day. Nowadays, the 'lamb bank' is a national service, and one of the best aids to the sheep industry in countless years. The three wise Cumbrians, who thought of the idea over lunch, are no longer with us but, as Gordon Savage, son of Matthew, commented, "Farmers up and down the country will always be grateful to them for their vision."

Changes there may have been in farming and in the methods and skills employed, but there is a traditional side which survives the passage of time, including annual outdoor events like shows and sheepdog trials. In fact, the "dog days", at Patterdale, Threlkeld and Rydal, have received a boost from tourism in the post-war years, while organisers of agricultural shows have seemingly grown in ambition and enterprise. Given men and women of drive and initiative, such as the husband-and-wife team of Ernie and Muriel Slee, long-service officials of the Skelton show society, small village events can swell into vast affairs on much bigger sites – parkland close to the Hutton-in-the-Forest mansion in the case of Skelton's ever-increasing exhibition. Thank goodness that they have not grown so much that they have lost their customary chumminess, as heard when loudspeaker announcements are spiced with dialect and, in many cases, first-name terms are used. Skelton is not alone in claiming that it has a friendly show.

While the shows go on and seem assured of long lives, some classes of competition have succumbed since the 1950s. The majesty of heavy horses, like Clydesdales, disappeared gradually as tractors took over on the farms, and gone, too, are the once-dominant cattle breeds, Shorthorns, Ayrshires and Friesians, with the arrival of fuller-fleshed European types.

The 170-year-old Penrith show was once dominated by Shorthorn cattle and described, year after year, as the "shop window" of the breed. Now, however, Shorthorns are reduced in numbers and rub shoulders with Charolais, Limousin and Blonde d'Aquitaines, as well as South American alpacas, Boer goats and Rouge de l'Ouest sheep.

Farmers, farm workers and their families were once most numerous in the crowds, but today's slicker, more modernised agriculture needs less in the way of labour. Something more cosmopolitan is appreciated by the countryfolk of today, calling for "special attractions", such as glistening displays of vintage motor cars, the breathtaking thrills of bungee jumping and pretty women showing off the latest fashions in dresses, coats and swimwear. An eye-catching feature of Skelton show, over many years, was the choice of a "Country Princess" from an array of gorgeous girls, many of them farmers' daughters.

So the July and August of every year can be a glorious time of activity in blissful surroundings – depending on the weather, of course. Some of the shows have had chequered careers, with stops

Lord Lonsdale (left) presents Edmund Harper, of Sedbergh, with his trophy for winning the championship for hand-made shepherds' crooks at Ullswater "dog day" at Patterdale in 1967. The Earls of Lonsdale have always supported the "dog day", famous for its sense of occasion and gorgeous setting.

and starts, according to variations in enthusiasm, but others have carried on solidly, apart from enforced breaks during the war years. Shows are evidence of the virility of community life and give a pleasant sparkle to the summer scene – precious treasures from a past age which should be guarded zealously.

In most cases, the local show first flourished in the tranquil years of the 19th Century. So it is now a beautiful piece of Victoriana, a day-long cameo of rural life, in which competitors are often the descendants of those of the past. Unpretentious and unflurried, the show is essentially a village get-together, with as much emphasis on socialising as winning prize tickets. Tucking into a salad lunch in a marquee, listening to the chatter and, possibly, fighting off a languorous wasp are among the delights of showday.

In the essential calendar of farming there were once several dates which had to be observed. Whitsuntide, in spring, and Martinmas, in autumn, marked the beginning and the end of workers' engagements on farms. Would they "stop on" for a further term or must the boss go into town to take on a new man or woman at one of the biannual hiring fairs?

The former significance of Candlemas Day (2nd February) has also dwindled. At one time that was the day on which farms were entered or vacated under tenancy agreements, as well as marking the end of the financial year when all accounts had to be settled and the interest on borrowed money became due. Weather pundits also attached some importance to 2nd February, saying:

> Candlemas Day, if it be fair,
> Half o' winter's to come an' mair.
> Candlemas Day, if it be foul,
> Half o' winter's gone at Yule.

Improved mechanisation has removed "tatie week" from the timetable. The week was once a holiday given by schools in October to enable the pupils to collect the potato crop – the dirty, back-breaking task of scratching the "taties" from the soil and chucking them into huge baskets. Clearing a big field of the crop could last several days, boys and girls cycling to and from the farm, morning and evening. During the war years, 1939-45, the acreage was doubled, if not trebled, and all hands were needed. While potato picking provided testing experience of the hard world ahead, there were some qualms about the wisdom of closing schools for this "holiday", as many children were receiving only a part-time education through having to share their premises with evacuees.

Westmorland Education Committee, in a neat Nelsonian touch, decided to keep schools open but agreed that their headmasters could turn a blind eye to the ruling, should farmers ask for older boys to be released to pick potatoes. For years it was the first experience of the workplace for youngsters in rural areas (and of pay, which never seemed to match the effort involved!).

Clipping of sheep continues on Lakeland farms, but the clipping days are not as colourful and eventful as those of more spacious days, before the war, when the feast which followed included a massive round of beef, a leg or two of veal and home-cured hams,

Vintage tractors on parade in the main arena of Skelton agricultural show in the 1980s. (*Frederick C. Wilson*)

and the merry-making went on into the early hours of the next morning. At farms like Gowbarrow Hall, by the side of Ullswater, the number of sheep clipped ran into the tens of hundreds. Fifty or sixty helpers took part, watched by a host of interested onlookers. After the war there were few big feasts and sing-songs – rationing put paid to them.

Farmers in the Eden Valley occasionally suffer from a rare phenomenon, the Helm wind of Cross Fell, a vicious blast of air, almost hurricane-like in its power, which occurs most frequently along the sixteen miles of the Pennine range between the villages of Melmerby and Warcop. A bar of cloud hanging over the Pennines is a sign to those further away that "the Helm is on".

Mr. Gordon Manley, a president of the Royal Meteorological Society, who made a special study of the wind conditions in the

Of the village agricultural shows in the Eden Valley, one of the most impressive is that at Skelton, near Penrith, held in a glorious setting at Hutton-in-the-Forest. For the centenary show in 1980, officials were suitably arrayed in Victorian attire. (*Frederick C. Wilson*)

1930s, from a hut between Cross Fell and Knock Fell, said that its desiccating and shrivelling effect on vegetation in springtime was to be feared. Accompanied by rain, the blast was known as "a wet Helm" but it was even more dangerous when accompanied by snow, for the driving could be phenomenal. Farmers must attempt to bring their sheep down to lower pastures to avoid heavy losses. Table Mountain, overlooking Cape Town, South Africa, has been cited as a case in which topographical features produce similar wind and cloud phenomena. The Helm bar, lying on or slightly above the crest of the Pennines, has been likened to the "tablecloth" of Table Mountain.

Some of the richest, fruitiest stories of agriculture in Cumbria concern the auction marts where livestock is sold – tales of banter between auctioneers and customers and of vendors' reluctance to accept the bids being indicated, some with the merest raising of an eyebrow or the minute lifting of the finger.

A fine parade of cattle at Penrith agricultural show. (*Frederick C. Wilson*)

Jack Proctor, a Penrith auctioneer of a past era, told of one frustrated farmer whose sheep he was selling at the little mart at Troutbeck, between Keswick and Penrith:

"Yan day – mebbee about 1950 – Ah was sellin' these laal black hoggs. Fit laal things – they wad lowp out for a bite o'grass.

"Ah sez, 'Ten shilling a hed, ten shilling a hed ... '

"T'owld farmer sez, 'Bad price, Jack. Bad price.'

"Well, Ah carries on and he pipes up agin, 'Bad price, bad price'.

"So Ah sez, 'Sell away, mun. Sell away. The way these laal things can lowp a dyke, thoo'll hev them back bi tomorrer'."

It was also at Troutbeck that the auctioneer was trying to sell an old sheep for a grizzled veteran; in fact, in Jack's words, its horns were so long that it was "vanyer blind".

"Just a young sheep," claimed the exasperated farmer, trying to whip up interest. Good auctioneers can assess the merits of an animal at a glance and Jack thought that he should make his views known on this particular sheep: "Aye," he shouted. "Seah young that Joe, here, larnt to clip on her." That put the record straight as to the age of the animal and produced a loud guffaw from the ranks of buyers.

Sales of livestock in country areas, mainly at the time of farmers' retirements, were marked by the provision of meals, generally sumptuous affairs, but sometimes lacking in finesse.

Auctioneers and customers were tucking into ham and pickles, bread and butter, when the farm cat jumped on the table, hoping for a titbit of food. The farmer's wife reacted angrily by pulling the spoon out of a big jar of mustard and rapping the cat on the backside. As the animal scuttled away, she turned to the diners, saying, "Yu'll hev some mair mustard, gentlemen."

Marts at Troutbeck, Appleby and Southwaite contributed to the local economy until they were closed. Those at Penrith, Kirkby Stephen and Lazonby survive and the prices paid there reflect the prosperity, and sometimes the anxiety, of the farming community over a wide district.

When a farmer offered for sale a Shorthorn cow in the old mart at Penrith, during the 1950s, he pulled from his coat pocket a bottle of whisky, brandishing it as he ushered the animal round the sale ring and calling out: "The buyer can have this instead of 'luck money'." With hard spirits scarcer than cash, he had hit a crafty diversion from the customary payback of a variable sum by vendor to purchaser, traditionally known as "luck money" and once seen as an essential adjunct to a sale. Time was when no farmer would have thought of selling a beast or a sheep without giving a "luck penny" – and no buyer would have failed to ask for it. The original idea was to provide the wherewithal to drink to the new purchase. Over the years, there have been moves to outlaw the practice, but old traditions die hard.

We live in an age of hustle and bustle. The insistent ring of the telephone disturbs snoozes and romantic moments. High-pressure salesmen pester us with hard-sell tactics and masses of junk mail. The computer rules business life, and costs many their jobs. Travel is a helter-skelter experience until, just occasionally, on a rural road, transport is brought to a halt by a flock of sheep being moved by men and dogs – and we have time to reflect. The skills of the shepherd are age-old skills, irreplaceable by modern technology, and for a few precious moments we are back to normality and tranquillity as sheep and lambs are urged along with old-time care – and not a computer in sight!

7

Last days of Lowther

For older Cumbrians, there is a special fascination about Lowther Castle. Although it was reduced to an empty shell in the 1950s, a mere mention of the castle whets the appetite for nostalgia. Local history is enlivened by effervescent stories about the glorious heyday of Lowther, the rich hospitality of the Earls of Lonsdale, the royal and noble guests and the massive meals, which were washed down with every kind of drink imaginable.

Of all the men who have held the title, Hugh Cecil, 5th Earl of Lonsdale, the famous Sporting Peer, probably enjoyed greater popularity than the rest. A glamorous and dynamic figure, he was generous in his patronage of a range of sports, and adventurous in his pursuit of personal achievements. As a gambling man, he once undertook to walk 100 miles along the Great North Road in 24 hours – and did it. Another contest involved completing four five-mile horse rides – one with a single horse, one with a four-in-hand and two with pairs. He donned the gloves with boxing champions and shot game on the Equator and in the Arctic Circle.

In the days of the 5th Earl, everything at Lowther Castle was done in the grand style. Lord and Lady Lonsdale and their closest friends sat on a dais during luncheon, overlooking the rest of their guests. Leading London hotels could not have been more stately in their service; silent-moving waiters, in dark indoor livery and with heads powdered, added to the impression of exemplary attentiveness.

All that ended when the Earl moved out of the castle after the Christmas of 1935, to spend the rest of his life in Rutland. After his death in 1944, he was brought back to Lowther church, close to the castle, for burial alongside his wife, Grace, who had passed away two years earlier. As a tribute to him, gardeners lined the grave with daffodils, so that not a fragment of newly-turned earth showed through as he was laid to rest. Yellow was, and is, the colour of the Earls of Lonsdale.

There can be few, if any, still alive who dined in Lowther Castle but some may remember visiting the lovely gardens which were sometimes open to the public. Hugh's Garden was a sight in itself, for there were eleven acres laid out to a plan which the 5th Earl brought back from Versailles. It took 30,000 bedding plants to fill the beds – dahlias, antirrhinums and East Lothian stocks. The rose garden was also magnificent, containing 20,000 blooms, and there were also the Japanese gardens, with still, silent, lily-covered ponds, Shinto temples and Japanese bridges.

The head gardener, James Jeffrey, devoted much time to the cultivation of gardenias, Lord Lonsdale's favourite buttonhole. Every day, wherever he travelled, his daily gardenia followed him from Lowther, carefully packed in moistened cotton wool. Once, when he went to South Africa for three weeks, James Jeffrey made up sufficient buttonholes for the full journey, kept fresh on ice on that occasion. In the heyday of Lowther Castle, Jeffrey supervised between thirty and forty gardeners.

The sale of the castle furnishings, over 21 days in the spring of 1947, marked the beginning of the end of a gallant epoch. Newspapers described the sale as "probably the largest of its kind ever held in the country". London and provincial antique dealers, some of them commissioned by American and European buyers, crowded into the castle. There were shining Rolls Royces amongst the cars lined up outside.

It was the last opportunity to see the ancestral home in all its splendour. Auctioneers Maple and Co. moved about the building to sell many of the lots *in situ*. Books were sold in the library and pictures in the picture gallery; the rostrum was moved to the state bedroom, where kings, queens and princes once slept, for the auctioning of homely things like wool mattresses, rush-seated chairs, bedsteads, writing tables and hangings from the bedroom walls. Northern dealers, with a keener sense of the past associations of Lowther Castle, often outbid London buyers. One London man

The pre-war grandeur of Lowther Castle, near Penrith, traditional home of the Earls of Lonsdale, on a day when the splendid gardens were open to the public. During the 1950s, the castle was gutted, so that only the shell remains.

said, "I can only think that it was the local historical and sentimental associations which caused prices to reach such high figures."

The sale proceeds, after 21 days of auctioneering, were around £140,000, a great deal of money in 1947. The rich and famous numbered among the buyers. Sir Alexander Korda, the film magnate, went in search of curios for use in "period" films. He bought some of the canary yellow broughams, phaetons and wagonettes, horsedrawn vehicles which were once a familiar sight in Penrith and the surrounding area. One of the broughams was purchased for display in the Belle Vue Gardens, Manchester. Sir Alexander was not the only screen personality to make a purchase. A collection of Hogarth prints was bought for £165 by Peter Murray Hill, the actor, whose wife, Phyllis Calvert, was a star of the silver screen.

Billy Butlin, the holiday camp entrepreneur, sent a representative who bought bookcases and several books (the latter "heavy going", ranging in subject from natural history to old coins). They were intended for the library of a new holiday camp at Pwllheli, said Butlin's man, adding, "We are trying to give our guests every-thing – not only fun and games but facilities to improve their knowl-edge and broaden their outlook. No doubt there will be students among the holidaymakers who will appreciate them." This seemed a surprising statement in 1947 – and is even more so half-a-century later!

The Earls of Lonsdale had an intriguing range of interests when reading. The books sold included the bloodthirsty "Art of Assassi-nating Kings", 1696, and there was an incongruously practical touch about "The Best Method of Curing White Herrings", for which somebody paid £2 10s (£2.50). Early editions of the work of William Wordsworth were bought for the Wordsworth museum at Dove Cottage, Grasmere, the poet's one-time home.

Heirlooms of five successive Earls of Lonsdale were included, but the most eye-catching were the treasures collected by the 5th Earl during his colourful life. Boxing belts recalled the days when "young Mr Lowther" challenged the great John L. Sullivan, the world heavyweight champion, in New York. Other trophies of an adventurous life were the heads of big game animals. Saddles from the Middle West, where he was, briefly, a cowboy in his youth, became numbered lots, as did dog harness from the Arctic Circle, used when Lord Lonsdale discovered gold in the Klondyke.

The castle's contents, gathered by generations of Lowthers from the four corners of the world, were dispersed almost as widely as the places they were brought from. Carpets from Turkey went to America; tapestries from Persia went to Norway, and Arctic tro-phies to Wapping. Quite apart from the purchases of the experts, hundreds of local folk secured souvenirs of the castle whose history was so entwined in local legend. A Penrith man, Robert Robertson, paid £42 for a carved oak sideboard because he was one of the men who had made it over 40 years before, as an apprentice cabinet maker with the Penrith firm of Joseph James, Ltd. By 1947, Mr Rob-ertson was the managing director. Another Penrith man, Jimmy Dias, handed over £5 10s. (£5.50) for a rare item – a pair of the long-toed dancing boots of Dan Leno, the music hall star of the 1890s.

Visitors to the spectacular gardens of Lowther Castle in the 1930s pause to admire a favourite pony led by the Earl of Lonsdale – the famous "Yellow Earl", a legegd in the history of Cumbria in general and sport in particular.

The art collection, covering two centuries, prompted the biggest prices of the sale, with 1,600 guineas and 1,500 guineas paid for pictures by noted painters of the Dutch and Belgian schools. At the other end of the price scale, many Lake District folk paid small sums for paintings just to remind them of the great days of Lowther, although journalist George Hobley's purchase was more meaningful, a water colour of the castle gardens painted by his father, E.G. Hobley, ARCA. Among the sculptures, prices ranged up from one guinea to 970 guineas, the latter for the figure of a Grecian lady, described by the buyer, a London antique dealer, as "a very beautiful and important Attic sculpture of the first half of the fifth century, BC".

For the big game trophies and treasures, most of them collected by the 5th Earl on his travels, prices ranged from £1 for a stuffed anteater or bear up to £11 for "swans complete with glass case". Two stuffed crocodiles were described as "a bargain" at £2. The sale ebbed and flowed; big prices were paid by big city experts and small, even tiny, amounts were handed over by Cumbrians who simply wanted to say, "That came from Lowther Castle," such was the sense of pride in the place.

On the final day, in May 1947, the last scraps were put up for sale. There were shouts of "Is it full?" when a 120 gallon whisky puncheon was offered. "Regretfully, no," replied auctioneer Thomas Wyatt. The cask was withdrawn because only a small price was bid. There was no bid at all for a Turkish bath, but an electric massage machine from Lord Lonsdale's bathroom went for £3 10s (£3.50). The last lot of all comprised six steel fenders, knocked down to a Mr Brooks for £2. It was all over.

There was intense interest in the future of Lowther Castle, now that it had ceased to be a nobleman's dwelling. One idea came from *Herald* editor Tom Sarginson ("Silverpen") when he wrote: "Cannot the Government, who are the only people who have any money in these doleful days, think of something spacious and splendid? What about a national agricultural college, with full-scale professorships in veterinary science and research and complete schools of forestry? Where would you ever find an estate better fitted for such a destiny? Our agriculture will have to be much more scientific in the future than it has been in the past, with its rule-of-thumb fumbling, and Lowther Castle could provide a complete University for the State."

Just how could the castle be preserved so that it might make a useful contribution to the 20th Century? Remember that it had been unoccupied since 1935 when, under the increasing burden of taxation, the 5th Earl chose to live in Rutland.

Then, in the war years of 1939-45, a purpose was found for the castle by the Army when it became the CDL School (initials standing for Canal Defence Lights) – a code-name for a secret establishment, under the direct control of the War Office, responsible for experimenting with a special searchlight for tanks. The vicinity of the castle was a scene of intense activity while this work was in progress. While the soldiers did not occupy the central part of the castle, they used both wings, which suffered in consequence.

It was on the grounds that the military occupation left its worst blemishes. The lawns and gardens, once so delectable, became a sorry scene of devastation, torn by the tracks of tanks and disfigured by ugly buildings.

The scars of war were still in evidence in the 1940s and 1950s while attempts were made to find a new use for the empty castle. Four Lancashire boroughs planned to join forces and turn the building into a school for educationally sub-normal children, but the idea had to be dropped because the Government refused to make grants towards the high cost of conversion. The proposed transformation of the castle into a police training college or a high quality museum, and schemes for a forestry school or an agricultural college, were also to fail. The great barrier was the very size of the castle.

Every endeavour was made to retain the building by the present Earl – James, the seventh holder of the title since it was recreated in 1807 – who resides at nearby Askham Hall. With utmost reluctance, he decided in 1956, that the castle should be largely demolished but that its handsome facade should be left standing as a lasting memorial to its illustrious past.

By April 1957, the final disintegration of the once-magnificent interior of the castle was well under way. Sales of fixtures, fittings and building materials were major steps towards the demolition. Prices ranged from a few shillings to £164. Although it was not as glamorous a sale as that of 1947, when the furniture, pictures and books were knocked down, some souvenir hunters turned up. A Durham historian, Mrs Phyllis Marshall, bought statues of Richard I and Edward III to give her "atmosphere" when she wrote about Edward and his descendants. Two bath-like articles, said to be ancient Egyptian coffins, were acquired by a Melton Mowbray man who planned to embody them in a new house. A staircase, panelling, flooring, stained-glass windows, ceilings and elegantly carved commode chairs were knocked down in 5½ hours of selling. Little bits of Lowther were soon on their way to new homes in all parts of the British Isles.

The outer shell remains to this day – a mute reminder of a one-time world of splendour and luxury, bounded by tapestried walls and warmed by blazing logs in great marble fireplaces.

Legend had it that there were as many rooms as there were days of the year. In fact, there were only 277.

Each year, in August, Lowther Castle is back in the spotlight during the Lowther horse driving trials and country fair, an event which has the triple attraction of an idyllic setting in rolling parkland, Royal patronage (in the person of the Duke of Edinburgh, formerly among the competitors) and a programme which caters for a wide range of interests and tastes, from ferrets to fishing, golf to gundogs, brass bands to bungee jumping.

This yearly supershow, based on rural pursuits, has overtaken older, more traditional events to put itself firmly at the head of Cumbria's calendar of crowd-pullers. Although horse-driving is the keynote, there was something of a "doggy" take-over in the 1990s. There are dog shows, dog races and dog food trade stands and, most of all, there are dogs. They come in all shapes and sizes – bouncy terriers, alert sheepdogs, jaunty Jack Russells, bristling bulldogs, disdainful dachshunds, pert pekingese and slinky, shapely whippets and Italian greyhounds.

The star of Lowther for many years has been George Bowman, a Penrith carpet dealer, whose mastery of horse driving has gained him many championships. A striking figure in a broad-brimmed hat, urging on his team of black Cumberland cobs, he has been the sport's national champion nineteen times and his total haul of medals and other awards verges on the phenomenal. The Duke of Edinburgh, as a rival but also as a team-mate in British teams in world and European events, once said: "George has a remarkable talent for putting horses together and making them do what he wants them to do."

Had George Bowman been a footballer achieving the same level of success, he would be a household name and received extravagant publicity, but the sport of carriage driving does not carry the same appeal for the masses. However, with others, he brings back to Lowther some old-time grandeur and glamour for a few days each August.

8

Charlie on the ball

Some reckon that there is a single minute, possibly less, which can determine the course of life of every individual, success or failure, happiness or misery. For Charlie Short, that brief decision-time occurred in 1946 during the lunch-break on a Carlisle building site. Conversation turned to local football when Charlie mentioned that he was hoping to find a club to play for. One of his mates recommended Penrith FC, as he had such pleasant memories of his time as a player there. Local fame and lifelong happiness stemmed from those few remarks.

There was just one snag. Charlie Short was a goalkeeper and Penrith did not need one. But they did want a hotshot centre forward – a goal-scorer rather than a shot-saver – and, on the suggestion of Gerald Sykes, the club chairman, Charlie agreed to make the positional move. With hindsight, the switch might well be seen as one of the most inspired decisions in the history of football. Within a year of becoming Penrith's centre forward, Charlie Short, then aged 26, was almost a legendary figure and the holder of a record which will surely stand for all time. Cheering crowds – for this was after the war and enthusiasm was sky high – saw him score 102 goals in the 1946-47 season, either with bullet-like headers or his much favoured right foot.

His feats were like something from a comic paper. Only a ficti- tious hero, such as 'Roy of the Rovers' could have matched Short's scoring powers. After he made the goalnet dance ten times in the first three matches, a local reporter penned this masterpiece of understatement: "The attack has been greatly strengthened by the inclusion of C. Short, a well-built, thrustful centre forward."

Footballing distinction was not the only result of Charlie's decision to play for Penrith. It was there that he met his wife, Ethel, they settled in the town and had two children, a son and a daughter. All in consequence of a lunch-time chat with a mate.

What great days those were in the sphere of soccer, with success, silverware and crowds of 2,000 to urge on the multi-talented team who never received a penny for their endeavours. Companionship and the joy of winning were adequate rewards. Loyalty was the keynote and players sensed a real pride in doing well for the club and for the town. The success was such in season 1946-47 that team selection was almost a formality. When Gerald Sykes and his committee met at the Horse and Farrier, in King Street, every Monday evening, somebody proposed, "Same team". The others echoed, "Same team", and they moved on to the next business on the agenda.

Changing rooms were at the Horse and Farrier. The players trooped through town streets, with overcoats slung over their blue and white strips, as they made their way to the field, their studded boots clattering over the pavements. After the final whistle, they raced each other back to the pub, hoping to be first into the tin bath, which had to be used by all 22 players and the referee in a yard behind the inn.

Penrith, the 'Bonny Blues', duly won the championship of their league and two knock-out competitions, one of them for the Cumberland Cup, a considerable honour which the club had never gained before. The triumphs of 1946-47 were generally ascribed to team spirit, a "one for all, all for one" feeling which sprang from the fact that most of the players had been in HM Forces during the war years.

Then there was the scoring potency of Charlie Short. He had a keen eye for an opening, the strength of build to resist most physical challenges and he kicked the ball with startling ferocity – so long as it was on his right foot. After scoring 102 goals in his first season, he took his tally to 220 in a little over three years with the club. However, the Penrith fan of the 1940s was a demanding fellow. As Charlie left the pitch one day, after totting up seven goals in the space of 90 minutes, one supporter complained: "By gum mate. You missed some chances today."

The famous Penrith team of the immediate post-war years, with their trophies. Front
(left to right): Freddie Stout, Brian Seery, Tommy Boustead, Cyril Branthwaite
(captain), Jackie Donaldson, Bob Snowdon, Arthur Docker. Standing (players only):
Arthur Bell, Charlie Short, Andy Forsyth, Ronnie Reay, John Bell.

The first three post-war seasons, covering from 1945 to 1948, saw a
glorious surge of triumph. So successful was the side which
"starred" Charlie Short, Tommy Boustead, Fred Stout, Ronnie Reay,
Jackie Donaldson and the Bell brothers, John and Arthur, that the
Penrith club decided on a bold move to leave local competition and
try their luck in the much stronger Northern League, centred on the
North East of England, which included powerful sides like Bishop
Auckland, winners of the FA Amateur Cup, the premier competition for small-town clubs.

But before the advance could be made there was much to be
done. Changing quarters in a pub were not acceptable to the hierar-
chy of the Northern League who insisted on there being dressing
rooms on the ground. The town's response to the challenge was
heartwarming, especially that of the football folk. As soon as season
1947-48 closed, supporters and committee-members hurried down
to the field on long summer evenings and worked until dusk on new
changing rooms. Bricklayers, plasterers, joiners and other crafts-

men all gave their services while less skilled men were their labourers and teaboys.

Local architect Frank Blanc, who designed the building, entered into the spirit of the time by giving back a large part of his fee as a donation. Similarly, builders provided cut-price materials; one of them was Bob Reay, a keen supporter, who erected the town's first post-war housing estate on Scaws.

The splendid new changing rooms were completed in time for the opening fixture in the Northern League in season 1948-49, a "plum", with Bishop Auckland to test the Penrith newcomers. Jubilation engulfed the town as "our lads" beat the famous visitors by two goals to one, thanks to Charlie Short's winning header. Rain lashed down but 2,000 turned up to see sporting history made.

You could find the Eden Valley sporting scene in the most unexpected of places. Travel along a country road in midsummer, turn a corner into a leafy lane and you might encounter two teams of footballers doing battle in a farmer's field, with up to a thousand spectators, sucking ice-creams and gossiping in the evening sunshine. Yes, summer soccer was almost the norm. In fact, it still is in some villages.

There were two football 'seasons'. Routine fixtures in local leagues, between August and April, represented the authorised version, while on summer evenings in June and July there were the rural 'medals', or knock-out competitions, in places like Crosby Ravensworth, Kings Meaburn, Bolton, Knock, Calthwaite, Kirkoswald and Great Strickland, which tended to be decidedly livelier, marked by parochial rivalries between neighbouring villages. The football authorities in London took a dim view of these out-of-season contests because the matches did not come under their control and were generally played on roughish pitches in farm fields, with inexperienced men as referees. League stars ignored the official ban, and knock-outs like the Waitby Cup, in villages around Kirkby Stephen in Upper Eden, drew bigger and bigger crowds as the rounds progressed, sometimes topping the 1,000-mark. The competition has now existed for 75 years.

There used to be a muck or nettles approach to the 'medals' and some of the players, in seasons long ago, endangered opponents by turning out in heavy clogs. However, cries from the crowd of "Kick him again, he's still breathing", after a player was injured, were intended to amuse, rather than incite.

The main winter competitions under the regime of the Football Association were the Penrith and District League, started in 1899, and the Eden Valley League, some village teams playing in both. The season's highspot was the P and D League's knock-out competition final, invariably played on the Penrith FC pitch on Easter Monday before noisy crowds of 2,000 and more. Spectators may not have been well versed in the finer points of the sport but made up for this with self-made favours, noisy rattles and verbal encouragement: "Shoot, Harry, yer gurt dribbling beggar ... Watch oot for yon fullback; he's a dirty —— ... Hey, will thoo keep on thi wing or ah'll kick thi —— ..."

A story used to be told that when Above Derwent played Keswick Red Rose in the P and D cup-final of 1905 the rival battle cries were "Up the kippers" and "Come on the tatie pots". The latter was in honour of Tom Boustead, a Braithwaite innkeeper who, as well as conveying the Above Derwent team to matches aboard his three-horse coach, used to provide generous tatie pot suppers. And the "kippers" cry was a facetious reference to Percy Todd, a Keswick fishmonger, who fostered football in that town for many years.

They did things in style in 1905, for the captain of the victorious Above Derwent was hoisted on to broad shoulders and, led by a brass band, the team and their supporters headed for a nearby hostelry to celebrate. Sadly, the old Penrith and District League faded out in the 1960s but changing lifestyles led to the setting up of a replacement, the Penrith and District Sunday League, in 1971.

Sporting tradition in the smaller communities of Eden and North Lakes lost some of its lustre in the years following the 1939-45 war through the gradual fade-out of sports meetings in the villages. Many of those meetings traced back to the last century; some originated as village picnics. The sports at Bampton were typical, having been started in 1899. The area is a remote and picturesque one of meandering lanes, small fields full of summer colour and divided by walls of hunks of stone, and a rugged backcloth of fell country. Some vintage direction signs, at junctions of the little roads, point the way to Mardale, even though the hamlet was submerged in the

Take that! Pillow fighters at the Mungrisdale sports, which are now defunct.

1930s when the Haweswater dam was built to create the reservoir which helps to slake Manchester's considerable thirst.

Bampton's annual sports day, a leisurely, informal affair, was totally in keeping with the rural setting. There were sprints, sack races and egg and spoon scampers for the children, cheered on by proud parents, but the main part of the programme brought in "professional" runners, jumpers, cyclists and wrestlers from nearby towns and villages, with a few from further afield. These men were normally shop assistants, farmers, shepherds, telephone engineers, council workers and gardeners but on summer Saturdays they became "professional" athletes because they competed for a few pounds at the little meetings. Sometimes, sports days clashed and the runners, having picked up a prize or two at one venue, jumped into cars and raced off to another meeting in the hope of increasing their earnings. The money was hard earned. So-called amateur athletes were known to have their expenses paid – and more.

With chests thrust forward, two sprinters breast the finishing line – a scene from the 1960s at Bampton sports, made up of Cumberland and Westmorland style wrestling, a race up and down a nearby fell, footraces and cycle races. Most village sports meetings are now less ambitious, confined to children's events in many cases.

It was on wrestling in the traditional style of Cumberland and Westmorland that Bampton sports built their reputation in the inter-war years. Hound trails (on which there was often a great deal of betting), fell races up and down Knipe Scar, and track events for runners and bikers made up the rest of the afternoon's programme. The track, hacked out of a farmer's field with scythe and lawn mower and marked out with small flags, left much to be desired but astute handicappers generally ensured good sport and close finishes. However, some competitors "ran for a mark" – didn't try too hard, in the hope that they would receive more favourable starts from the handicapper on future sports days.

Spectators relished the ringside "crack" as much as they did the races. There were homely touches like meals made by local WI ladies and a dance in the village hall at night to a local band.

It was remarkable that smallish communities, the likes of Croglin, Dufton, Knock, Skelton, Armathwaite, Mungrisdale and Pooley Bridge, sustained sports meetings for as long as they did. Although some villages, such as Bampton, still put on races for the children, they are just pale shadows of the meetings of yesteryear. Likewise, bigger sports days, at Penrith and Keswick, have also succumbed to the brave new world of television, cheaper travel and holidays in faraway places.

Gone are the squire, the local headmaster and the vicar acting as judges and timekeepers for a day, and the bellman and the sports commentators who kept the programmes moving with bell or loudspeaker.

Sports enjoyed by individuals, such as golf, swimming and cycling, all have long histories and still flourish, but some old-time favourites, quoiting and old penny pitching, are virtually forgotten now. And nobody can possibly remember that baseball, American-style, was once played at Penrith – by teams of Canadian soldiers who were stationed there at the end of the 1914-18 war.

"The body swerve champion" was the first Penrith sportsman to go to London to play in a final. If the description is bewildering, Don Watson, a burly, middle-aged rabbit catcher, was a darts player who threw his arrows with a distinctive swerving motion of the upper body, a movement so pronounced that Bert Martin gave him the title in his reports in the *Penrith Observer*.

Watson was among the local experts of the game for many years but his hour of glory came in 1951 when his hours of practice at the Museum pub, in Castlegate, Penrith, enabled him to become North of England champion in the annual competition run by the *News of the World*. Ahead lay the chance of even greater glory in the national finals at Earl's Court, London. He was well supported on the big occasion. The Museum hired a 40-seater motor coach and seats were quickly booked up. Crates of beer were also loaded in case there was not enough time for several stops to be made for refreshment, along the way. Most of the travellers went to the final but for others the outing was a first-ever visit to London and they went to see the sights.

"The body swerve champion" won the first "leg" of his contest with F. Curtis, the Western Counties title-winner, only to lose the next two and make an early exit. Roland Nicholson, the landlord of the Museum, was adamant that the atmosphere of the final was "unreal". His man always flourished with two or three pints aboard, in pub surroundings. But on a stage and without several glasses of ale to lubricate his throwing arm, he lost his nerve – and the match.

Of all the games which have gained in popularity since the war, few can match dominoes. Only a pub pastime, say the purists, but that does not lessen the appeal. The principal pre-Christmas events used to be whist drives, for which prizes of whisky, turkey and goose were awarded, but festive domino drives ousted them years ago. An elderly Penrith couple play dominoes every morning, the agreement being that the loser makes lunch!

When pubs *were* pubs – dominoes at the Robin Hood, Penrith, in the 1950s. From left to right are: (unknown); Kitty Blenkinship; Bob Jackson; Mr Blenkinship (miller at Southwaite Green Mill); Jackie Brown.

9

Cricket to relish

A one-time MP for Penrith, J.W. Lowther, once said of cricket in the last century: "Cumberland is not what you might call a cricketing county. The configuration of the soil does not lend itself very favourably to very level cricketing grounds and the state of the atmosphere does not conduce to rapid pitches, on which quick scoring can be achieved.

"To give you an idea of the difficulties in which cricket in the county is pursued, I would mention that on one occasion, in a match I remember, a covey of partridges rose from between the wickets."

Partridges no longer flutter about the cricket fields of Cumbria – but, over the years since the second war, the summer game has been enriched by colourful characters and the spice of surprise and humour.

Arthur Rose, one of the bowlers of the Nunwick (Great Salkeld) club in the 1950s, was racing in to send down his next delivery. Suddenly and inexplicably, he veered to the left and, without breaking stride, ran towards the edge of the closely-cut central area, beyond which lay normal farm field conditions, grassy tufts, tree stumps, cow dung and all.

Startled fielders and batsmen were mystified until Arthur drew back his bowling arm and, with all the power he could muster, flung the ball into the outfield – just missing a scuttling rabbit which had dared to venture across the ground. Sometimes, after an afternoon in the outfield at one of these rural matches, players returned to the pavilion with several fresh mushrooms in their caps.

The Eden Valley's enthusiastic village cricket clubs include two neighbouring rivals in Culgaith and Temple Sowerby. Here, Tony Whitfield (Culgaith) knocks back the off stump of Temple Sowerby's Sam Prokas. A shot from 1977. (*Eric Davidson*)

The Cumbrian cricketer is a phlegmatic fellow, not given to displays of emotion and anger. Seldom are tempers frayed to a point where equanimity and control are lost – but it does happen.

The annual "medals" competition on the delightful, tree-surrounded ground at Appleby, nestling in a bend in the River Eden, provided many hours of evening entertainment. Two top teams of "pot-hunters", one composed of policemen, the other containing quality cricketers from in and around Penrith, took part in a keen contest.

Much of the enjoyment of these matches depended on the ability of the umpires who were kept busy adjudicating on a succession of appeals from the bowlers, alleging that batsmen were "run out" or, more frequently, "leg before wicket". If all these pleas had succeeded, the "medals" matches would have been of very brief duration.

During the constabulary's innings at Appleby, the cry of "How's that?" went up repeatedly, especially from a veteran of many such campaigns, known by the nickname of "Bunny" – but all to no avail. Frustration welled up but it seemed that the umpire *must* agree when a batsman stepped in front of his stumps and a ball from "Bunny" rapped him on the pads. He turned to the umpire in renewed triumph. "HOW IS THAT THEN?" he yelled, as slip fielders and wicket-keeper threw up their arms to strengthen the justice of his appeal. The official was not moved. "Not out," he barked. "Bunny" was astounded. He recoiled in disbelief. Hands on knees, he gazed at the ground, a study in absolute dejection.

The batsmen, meanwhile, saw the opportunity to steal a run, as the ball had struck the pads of one of them and a "leg-bye" could be taken. Despite the furore of the failed appeal, a fielder seized the ball and threw down the stumps, as one of the policemen struggled to make his ground.

This time the cry of "HOW'S THAT?" was even louder and more determined. But, as though decided on a permanent course of refusal, the white-coated umpire turned down the plea. This was too much for "Bunny". To carry on with the contest seemed pointless to him.

"Right lads," he called out. "We've had enough of this. We're off."

Summoning his men to follow with a wave of the arm, he strode purposefully towards the pavilion. Seven or eight cricketers followed; the Appleby "medals" competition had its first strike.

It lasted all of a minute. Wiser counsel prevailed in the person of a local council official, who pursued his dissatisfied team-mates, shouting, "Come on back, you silly ... ."

Reluctantly, the fielders retraced their steps, the game got going again and the policemen gained a handsome win over their dispirited opponents, by now reduced to total silence.

Just occasionally, local cricket found its way into the national press, generally because of some remarkable feat. In the 1950s a Stainton CC bowler, Brian Hill, performed a local 'first' by taking a wicket with each delivery of a six-ball over. Teenage batsman Tim McVey followed him into the headlines, many years later, by scoring two centuries in the course of a day, the first for Penrith Grammar School in the morning and the second for the third eleven of the Penrith club during the afternoon.

Players of less repute suddenly found themselves the centre of newspaper interest for more frivolous reasons, such as the Penrith batsman who set himself on fire when he fell, igniting the box of matches in a trousers pocket.

"Medals" games, limited to twenty overs of batting per side, with restrictions on how long each bowler could operate, were often preferred to the more formal Saturday afternoon matches. There was a bonus for spectators in the lively banter directed at players from the sidelines by witty onlookers like Jackie Lancaster whose wisecracks probably drew more people to the Penrith matches than the cricket itself.

The playing of local cricket has an enduring quality but, it seems, spectator-interest is slowly fading away. Onlookers are mainly elderly but are fiercely loyal, seldom missing a match, despite the handicaps of bad weather, disability or both.

Old habits die hard in the cricket fraternity in personal preferences for viewpoints. Strangely, some of the most loyal supporters rarely, if ever, enter the Penrith ground, preferring to stand on the outside of the street wall with contemporaries, like generations before them. Conversation on the sidelines can be entertainment in itself, often laced with the local vernacular:

"Noo then lads, this could be a canny finish. Could ga owther way."

"Aye, oor lads could manish it if they put bat t' baw. Wi need t' git on wit job."

"Well hit, but leuk he's got hisel cowt. A helluva catch, yan hand."

"Aye, wi need t' play it stiddy, yer knaw. Better a draw than give wickets away."

"We's in next then? Oh, nut him. Th' should hev sent in yan with a bit mair beef. This lad can barely hit it oft middle."

"Nut ser fast wid yer wards. Leuk, he got a laal bit tickle on't baw and it shot past t'stumper and doon t'boondry."

"Aye wiv won t' job. Good game o' cricket. Dusta think we desairve a drink efter si much excitement?"

The Eden Valley of Cumbria is one of the lesser known areas of cricketing enthusiasm, stretching from the Pennines in the east to the Lake District in the west, Kirkby Stephen in the south to Carlisle in the north. The grounds are visually splendid and the clubs are rich in tradition.

Among the delectable cricket fields of Upper Eden is the Hills Bottom ground of the Kirkby Stephen club, where this picture was taken during a children's match.

Village clubs are now welded together in the Eden Valley League, centred on Penrith, although their history goes back far into the last century. The country squires of Eden fielded teams of workers to play their neighbours among the landed gentry, with a few side-bets to enliven the proceedings. In some cases those old-time rivalries blossomed into clubs which now play in the league. The influential families who encouraged the game included the Earls of Lonsdale at Lowther, the Musgraves at Eden Hall, the Thompsons at Nunwick, the Vanes at Hutton-in-the-Forest, the Broughams at Brougham and the Parkers at Skirwith.

Over a hundred years ago the south front at Lowther Castle was a spectacular setting for the game, with much feasting and drinking. When Penrith played there in 1866 and allowed the home batsmen to pile up a massive score, the local newspaper reported: "Whether from the effects of the strong Lowther ale, or from a conviction that the match would not be played out, or from both cases combined, certainly the Penrith fielding became wilder and wilder."

Cricket matches were considerable social occasions in those far-off days. Plenty of food and drink and the presence of pretty and elegant ladies all contributed to the enjoyment. Press reports sometimes included details of the menus and lists of the gentry in attendance. Military bands occasionally provided musical accompaniment.

Lowther cricketers now play close to the village of Lowther, rather than the castle. There are special ground rules if the ball strikes a stately tree which grows in the middle of the field. For many years Lowther's secretary and scorer was John Peel, a direct descendant of the famous huntsman of the same name.

One country squire, R. Heywood Thompson, turned out for the earliest teams at Nunwick (Great Salkeld), along with members of his family, but his main contribution was to engage cricketers of skill as workers in the household or on the estate. They included Arthur Ruell and J. Kennan, who laid and cared for the pitch, and Ben Barrell and Sydney Lillywhite, both fine cricketers. Barrell, a demon bowler, was later to play for Lancashire, while Lillywhite was the son of a renowned Sussex and All England player.

Cricket once played a part in some agricultural shows, as at Crosby Ravensworth in the 1880s. A report said: "A match between eleven gathered from Crosby, Morland, etc. against the Appleby club was played. The villagers were much too strong for the 'cracks' from the county town and disposed of them for a very small score which was quickly run off before four wickets had fallen."

Similarly, the village flower shows, such as those at Temple Sowerby and Greystoke, were enlivened by cricket, with the more powerful Penrith club often invited to provide the opposition. The Howard family of Greystoke Castle were keen supporters of the game, although cricket has not been played in the village for over half-a-century.

Cricket still flourishes at Temple Sowerby, once described as "the Queen of Westmorland villages", midway between Penrith and Appleby on the A66. It was the cricketers of Temple Sowerby who figured in a strange stoppage in 1992. Playing at Workington in a Cumbria League match, the village batsmen were in sight of victory in a tense finish – twenty runs needed, five overs to go and two wickets standing. However, their concentration was broken by a pitch invasion by youths taking part in Workington's Uppies and Downies ball game, an annual outbreak of local tribal warfare dating back several centuries. Umpires halted play while the field was cleared of the unruly young men but the damage had been done and Temple Sowerby's victory bid was thwarted.

There have been other unusual interruptions of play, such as fielders dashing away to answer fire alarms. A batsman at Edenhall was going well and seemed likely to make a big score until he insisted on retiring – he had to get back to the farm to milk the cows.

Another peculiar hiatus, which attracted the attention of the newspapers many years ago, occurred on the village ground at Morland when a passing heifer tried to eat a pair of braces, belonging to one of the players. The hungry animal was eventually persuaded to disgorge – to the relief of the owner of the heifer, as well as the owner of the braces.

A cricketer was playing for the Stainton club when he had to dive out of the way of a passing hang glider which missed him by only a few feet! Bad flight stopped play, you could say. Aerial invaders also struck at Carlisle when umpire Arthur Stamper had to make a snap decision while aircraft of the famous Red Arrows gave a spectacular display of manoeuvres over the Edenside ground. He promptly removed the bails and stopped play until the pilots completed their breathtaking exhibition, only 100ft above the ground.

East Cumbria's quaintest cricket ground used to be at Gamblesby, a village at the foot of the Pennines which could once field a team consisting largely of members of the Little family. The ground fell away steeply on one side of the pitch, so that it was a masterpiece of anticipation if an outfield catch was taken. On the other side the wicket was close to a wall, so that ground rules applied – two runs if a shot struck the wall, four if it landed in the next field. In the 1960s the Gamblesby ground was levelled and the uniqueness removed. Another feature was the excellence of the teas provided in a farmhouse kitchen, little more than a six-hit from the field.

Newspaper files tell of many peculiar cricket encounters. The Penrith club once played a team of clowns who were putting on a show in town. A Kirkby Stephen eleven annually took on 22 shopkeepers, and the Appleby team used to face all-female opposition, the men's handicap being to bowl left arm and bat with broom-sticks.

In a county with more hills than flat fields Cumbria's cricketers have picked some of the most delectable parts of the countryside for their grounds, with backdrops of the Pennines, the Lakeland fells or the lushness of the Eden Valley. The Patterdale ground has magnificent views over the mountains at the head of Ullswater but there are many other fields of rustic charm and beauty, such as those at Culgaith (with the Pennines in the background), Caldbeck (more famous as the birthplace of huntsman John Peel), Staffield and Morland.

On one side of Caldbeck's neat, well-tended field is a vegetarian restaurant in the old Priests' Mill which provides a grandstand view of play in progress – while diners may eat sticky toffee pudding or Christmas pudding with rum sauce. There can be few eatinghouses in the land which offer such a mixture of seasonal delights!

One of the most successful of the old-established Eden Valley village clubs is that of Edenhall, a few miles from Penrith. The club owes its existence to the Musgrave family who lived at nearby Eden Hall until the mansion was demolished in the 1930s. As well as providing the field, they placed coins on top of the stumps beyond the boundary, to be given to batsmen who managed to smite the ball that far. Two Edenhall cricketers advanced to the first-class game in the 1980s in Graham Monkhouse, who spent several seasons with Surrey, and Paul Nixon, the Leicestershire, Kent and England A wicket-keeper.

Some of the village cricket fields of the past, such as those at Stainton and Millhouse, provided grazing for sheep and cattle for much of the week. Although the livestock was driven off on Saturdays before stumps were pitched, the cricketers' clean-up operations were rarely completely effective.

Peter Sarjeant, a one-time Penrith captain, was in a team of auctioneers who played a team of Ullswater farmers in a field at Watermillock, beside the lake. On going to bat, he glanced round the opposition fielders, noting to his surprise that there were twelve, rather than the permitted eleven. When he mentioned this to the wicketkeeper, he was assured that "Old Joe", an elderly man, stationed among the slip fielders, was not taking part; he liked to stand fairly close to get a better view of play!

All Cumbria cricket used to be "friendly". Or perhaps that's the wrong word to use, in view of some of the fall-outs involving decisions by inexperienced or excessively biased umpires. From the 1950s onwards all clubs moved over to leagues. Local trendsetters were the cricketers of Penrith who in 1951 abandoned their old programme of friendly matches with neighbouring clubs and others as far away as Barnard Castle and Dumfries. On entering the more demanding sphere of league cricket they relished a phenomenal run of success by lifting the championship of the Cumberland Senior League five times in their first eight seasons, 1951 to 1958, before advancing to the even stronger North Lancashire League, centred on Barrow-in-Furness.

At the start of this era of cricket glory the players changed into their whites in a small green hut of ancient construction. The cramped accommodation was not in keeping with the club's new status. In 1952 Jim Bowman, a big hitting batsman, set about improving matters with an inspiring speech at the annual meeting. Bowman gave a lead to lazier clubmates in setting off, single-handed, to dig the foundations in a corner of the cricket field, but his zeal was infectious. By 1956 Penrith CC had a smart new pavilion, the envy of cricket in the county, and more improvements have followed at regular intervals.

Penrith CC had a post-war swashbuckler in Harold Millican, a left-handed batsman with a keen eye, blacksmith's forearms and a considerable panache when at the wicket. His bat swishing like a scimitar, he was an outstanding run-getter on the Tynefield Park ground, although not all of his shots were out of the coaching manual. His scoring monopolies were typified by a match with Barnard Castle in the 1950s, in which the Penrith total raced to 100; no sooner had the tin plates been attached to the little scoreboard to announce this fact than Millican's personal century was being applauded – he had made almost all the runs scored. He brought added lustre to the club when he gained the captaincy of the Cumberland and Westmorland county side who played some of their Minor Counties matches on the Penrith ground, then a field among fields in open countryside but now surrounded by schools and bungalows in the expanding town.

10

Age of the horse

Eyes swivelled, chatter subsided and pulses quickened as a shimmering black stallion with a teenage lad astride, raced through the crowds. A man cried out: "Hey up, how's that for a hoss? Look at him ga. Theer's yan to fill the eye."

The scene was a long strip of waste land, running parallel with the A66 road in Upper Eden, an ordinary enough patch of ground for most of the year, but which took on colour and life in the raw for three or four days each autumn, on the occasion of Brough Hill fair. Beneath a constant haze of camp fire smoke lay a sea of caravans, stalls, tents and faces – a scene which had been re-enacted year after year since Edward III granted the fair a charter around 1330. Every few minutes, the thud of hooves and the raised voices of the dealers split the crowds, as steeds of all types and ages were raced back and forth: "There's a horse for you ... ".

The coats of the horses glistened like satin. Bare-back riders showed off the paces of their mounts in short bursts of frenzied activity, racing to and fro. Once at the very heart of activity on Brough Hill at fair-time, the presence of galloping horses and bargaining, hand-slapping men diminished slowly over the years. The fair survives – but only just.

Much more enduring is the inappropriately named Appleby New Fair every June (still 'new', although its history stretches back over the centuries). Like Brough Hill, Appleby has seen a drop in horse numbers but the general aura of fair life is more vigorous: opulent, glittery modern caravans contrasting with the traditional hooped wagons, many of them bedecked with cut-glass and Crown Derby china, old men with slouchy lurcher dogs, hundreds of sightseers. What is a holiday for thousands of gypsies and potter-folk is a grand spectacle for the locals.

Continuing zest for the Appleby gathering contrasts with the dwindling nature of Brough Hill which seems to be sinking slowly towards eventual oblivion. In the past the New Fair was repeatedly condemned by councillors and health officers who feared epidemics resulting from the yearly influx of up to 6,000 campers, because of a lack of adequate water supply and proper sanitation - faults which have now been remedied to some degree. These fears, plus cases of trespass on grazing land, damage to fences and failure to close gates, so that farm stock strayed, meant that on several occasions the Sword of Damocles was poised over the fair. Unruly behaviour was another threat, for the campers not only "drank the pubs dry" but sometimes caused trouble and aggression, once considered bad enough to be termed a "riot".

Long gone is the impressive sight of powerful horses, pulling long, flat carts, setting out from the railway station to deliver goods to town centre shops in Penrith. Each year British Rail gave prizes for the best groomed animals.

In villages the trend is much the same. Once, the clip-clop of horses might herald a milk delivery. Housewives walked to garden gates, with jugs in hands for the bland fluid to be poured into them from gill or pint measures. If, during the waiting time, the horse co-operated, a dash was made for the coal shovel and the rose bed was enriched with farmyard manure.

Farm workers, with pipes going, crouched behind the reins as their carts made a majestic progress down village streets, carrying loads of turnips or tottery piles of hay. The post-war rise in the use of tractors put an end to all that and sealed the fate of the blacksmith, once essential to the rural scene.

In the heyday of the farm horse in the Upper Eden village of Warcop, a thousand new shoes were fitted in a year. At the smithy, father and son James and Gilbert Hodgson also made and repaired harrows, ploughs and hand-rakes. There were cartwheels to hoop, plus the forging of all kinds of horse gear, hames, chains, crooks, clog irons and pig irons.

"There were many more farms then than now," said Gilbert Hodgson. "Some of them were quite small but they all needed a

horse or two, Shires or Clydesdales. Fitting four new shoes generally took around an hour – the removal of the old ones, dressing the
feet and putting on the new shoes."

Gilbert Hodgson's sixty-year career at the Warcop smithy ended
with his retirement in 1988 at the age of 73, but if you chat with the
old man, you can flit back to a more leisurely age when the village
street echoed to the ring of the blacksmith's hammer on the anvil
and the whinny of horses awaiting shoeing.

Cumbrian agricultural shows always featured classes for
sprightly Fell ponies, stately heavy horses and elegant hunters,
often made more eye-catching by lady riders in hard hats and sleek
jodhpurs. At Penrith show in 1947 there were seventeen classes for
heavy horses, ranging from filly foals to geldings of four years and
upwards, and classes for hunting horses, Fell ponies and riding
ponies. A prince among writers on agricultural topics, Robert
Burne, penned these paragraphs about the heavy horses at the village agricultural show at Skelton in the 1930s:

**"Where except Skelton could one imagine a horse class of
old favourites. Each horse has a special badge, as if it were
already a champion and each bears around its neck a
ribbon with a printed card appended, giving its age and
history. Who except the Skelton society would go to all the
trouble of printing a special card, shaped to the neck, for
each horse. But this is Skelton showmanship.**

**"Eldest of the twelve old nags is entered by Mr J. Millican,
Icold, Greystoke. This is what the horse's card says,
'Thirty-three years old, bred by Mr Thompson, Plumpton
Head. The parish horse. Done everything this summer, led
all the hay and does all the carting. Been in perfect health
all his life'.**

**"No formal report does justice to Skelton show. It is as
different from other shows in Cumberland as chalk is from
cheese. There is a life about it – and it certainly proved the
old adage that nothing succeeds like success."**

The changing scene in agriculture, just after the war, was
reflected in the advance of the tractor, as advertised in the newspa-

HRH The Duke of Edinburgh negotiates a tricky obstacle while competing in the horse-driving trials in Lowther Park. *(Frederick C. Wilson)*

per columns in the late-1940s. The Ford Motor Company, of Dagenham, advocated the Fordson Major – "the tractor with a PLUS, becomes a compact, 3-furrow ploughing unit". A few weeks later, farmers were told that an attractive batch of 50 Ferguson tractors had arrived in Carlisle and were in the showrooms of the main dealers – "the ideal vehicle for the small owner, to whom it has now become available through the relaxation of the permit regulations ". And the Ministry of Agriculture's advisory service, NAAS, offered to help with caring for tractors and planning tractor work on farms.

It was the beginning of the end for farm horses, although for some years they worked side by side with tractors in ploughing competitions promoted by societies at Cliburn, in the Eden Valley, and Skelton. At Cliburn in 1947 two cups were won by Norman Davidson, a horse ploughman, aged only 15, which suggested that old horses and old skills might survive for a few years more.

There was something refreshing about ploughing events, particularly the sight of real craftsmen and the smell of newly-turned turf. The skills were largely those of local farmers and farmworkers,

Come Back to Eden

although the entry lists also included such crack ploughmen as Tom Dixon, of Billingham-on-Tees, who claimed to have won 263 championships in a long career, and James Morrow, a former Irish champion. There were vast prize lists which meant that, although some of the top men took the trophies, the locals had an opportunity to win some of the lesser awards – for the best work by a David Brown tractor or a Ford Ferguson outfit, the finish most suitable for a binder, the neatest "ins and outs", the oldest and the youngest ploughmen.

Row upon row of powerful Clydesdales drawing ploughs across massive fields, leaving in their wake beautiful furrows with razor-edged top lines, made a sight to behold. Tractors gradually displaced the mighty steeds but machines could never have the same appeal for hawk-eyed enthusiasts who watched the work, inspected the sets and commented wryly on adjudicators' decisions.

Just after the 1939-45 war, the summer scene of the Northern Lakes and the Eden Valley was enlivened by a crop of field days, with fancy dress parades, motor cycle races, clay pigeon shoots, horse sports and wrestling, some of them to raise funds for village halls and playing fields. Youngsters with ponies had a rare old time taking part in the gymkhanas, composed of jumping competitions and a variety of races with fascinating names – potato, apple, Gretna Green, wheelbarrow, water-carrying, costume and musical tyres. Names differed but the qualities called for were exactly the same – nippy ponies and agile riders.

The names of most of those juvenile "stars" – T. Clark, Penrith; P. Smith, Hunsonby; Miss Alice Wales, Raughton Head; M. Wardropper, Kendal, among others – are forgotten, but one of them is better known than ever. George Bowman, winner of pony scampers, apple and potato races in the 1940s, is now the most successful competitor in the sport of four-in-hand horse team driving, voted "Carriage driving personality of the year" no fewer than nine times.

George Bowman, a successful carpet dealer, with a big shop in Penrith, recaptured the romanticism of a past age when, in 1972, he became the first man since the 1800s to drive a stagecoach from Edinburgh to London, a distance of almost 400 miles, sponsored by

Well-groomed horses and a shining carriage. This placid picture reflects the charm and appeal of the annual horse driving trials and country fair in the grounds of Lowther Castle. *(Frederick C. Wilson)*

a leading whisky distillery to raise money for charity. Twenty-two horses were used – five teams of four and two spares – and the aura of coaching was recalled by the sound of the posthorn, big receptions along the route and a greeting at journey's end from the Lord Mayor of London. "It was a wonderful trip," said George.

Time was when Penrith had its own racecourse on a spectacular sweep of land above the town, now the golf course. Betting men turned up in numbers to try to pick the winners of two-mile races over hurdles, named the Edenhall plate, Carleton plate, Inglewood hunt cup, Lowther plate and farmers' and tradesmen's plate.

As the years passed, however, the racegoers' conduct aroused public condemnation, as some were fraudsters and pickpockets. The meetings disappeared from the calendar around the close of the 19th Century after one of them was criticised in strong terms: "The county families and representatives of Penrith trade was conspicuous by their absence and the attendance was largely made up of that hungry multitude of hobbledehoys and loafers who live on the border-land between impecuniosity and starvation. The betting fraternity was an embodiment of blatant blackguardism and unhung humanity rarely to be met with in such abundance."

A glimpse of the turmoil of Appleby New Fair as a high-stepping horse shows off its paces. A picture from the 1970s – though the scene is re-enacted every year. *(Gordon Wood)*

On the credit side, some notable racehorse trainers have worked in Eden. Penrith-born R. W. Armstrong had stables at Eamont Bridge and Clifton before moving to Middleham, Yorkshire, and establishing a national reputation which was carried on by his descendants.

In more recent times Gordon Richards set up stables in the village of Greystoke and enjoyed much success over 30 years, including two winners of the Grand National, "Lucius" in 1978 and "Hallo Dandy" in 1984. Other Eden trainers, Jonjo O'Neill and Maurice Barnes, both originally achieved fame as jockeys, Barnes riding "Rubstic" to victory in the Grand National in 1979. On the evening of his triumph his local – the Fox Inn at Ousby – ran out of champagne!

11

The shows

Fun and games came to Penrith at Whitsuntide and Martinmas in the form of "the shows". In most places they would use the word "fair" but to people in and around Penrith the stalls, sideshows, merry-go-rounds and other entertainment, manned by raucous men and jolly women, were always "the shows".

The Great Dockray square was transformed from Saturday until Tuesday and, as children in the 1940s, we headed there in our hundreds. We did not always have many pennies to spend but found rare excitement and fascination in the noisy crowds, the thud of colliding dodgem cars and the whirl of 'The Whip' whose passengers screamed and clung to each other as the little cars hurtled round at high speed.

At the roll-a-penny stall a man called out:

"On the line the money's mine,
On the square I'll pay you fair".

We chanced a few precious coins, using one of the wooden chutes placed on the outside edge of the stall's surface which was divided into coloured squares marked 2,3,4,6 and 9. If we were lucky and the wobbling penny finally subsided on one of the squares, clear of the dividing lines, the attendant whizzed back the appropriate number of coins, by way of reward. We generally had another go, but soon realised that this form of gambling yielded only a brief thrill. Pocket money was quickly lost.

"The shows" always coincided with term time when farm workers came to town in search of new jobs at the hirings (unless they had been invited to "stop on" by their current employers and were happy to do so). Whether looking for work or not, lads and lasses travelled into town from remote farms for a rare taste of urban fund.

There was a double celebration at Whitsuntide so far as Penrith was concerned. Big Whit Tuesday was dedicated to the hiring of farm servants and Little Whit Tuesday, a fortnight later, was deemed to be for farmers' wives and children, who had missed the earlier merry-making. However, the word "little" was misleading, as the Great Dockray fair was just as big as on the earlier occasion, with coconut shies, shooting galleries, an obstinate punch-ball and the usual sideshows and stalls for people who were prepared to throw their money away.

Fat ladies drew circles of popeyed admirers, while there were competitive challenges in the coconut shies, "Aunt Sallies" and dart throwing. The boxing booth was always popular, with brawny farm lads willing to have a crack at the professional pugilists, generally after boosting their confidence with three or four rums or whiskies in the nearby White Horse or Two Lions. Some of them were half-drunk by the time battle commenced.

Tom Sarginson, a long-serving editor of the *Cumberland and Westmorland Herald*, wrote of the fairs: "They had an element of the picturesque; the very streets were a carnival of barbarian colour and the sun-lit or fog-filled squares of the old town of Penrith a favourite rendezvous for wonderful dreams of gilded magnificence.

"Even the entrances to the palatial abodes of the two-headed wonder, the lady of marvellously obese proportions, the lovely mermaid 'all the way from the South Sea Islands' and other freaks – or frauds – were more like the entrance to the fabled cave of Aladdin than anything else, where dazzling beings in dresses bespangled with iridescent sequins, and their faces upholstered with several layers of paint – and, I regret to say, a strata of dirt – danced beneath a flaring flambeaux of sputtering paraffin."

There was a strong hint of the sordid mixed with the gaiety of the Penrith "shows" in Victorian times. As well as bearded women, skeletal men and Dick Turpin with his matchless steed, men sang risqué songs in the streets in the hope of selling the sheets of naughty words. The case of the Continental Museum of Female Beauty went before the town's magistrates following the Whitsuntide fair in 1899. So disturbed was Police Sergt. Illingworth

A flashback to the colourful days when one of Penrith's squares, Great Dockray, was the setting for fairs – with dodgem cars, displays of strength, darts and roll-a-penny stalls – at Whitsuntide and Martinmas. *(Alec Fraser)*

when he saw pictures with titles like "The bride's first night", "An artist's model" and "A lady taking a bath" that two show proprietors, Edward Sherran and John Cooper, were later summoned and fined £1 and ten shillings (50p) respectively for putting on indecent shows.

Charles Allan, defending solicitor, could not understand the concern of the policemen and other witnesses. "The pictures have been on display for years and this is the first time anybody has found fault," he commented. "The class of people who visit the shows are not little girls from boarding schools but girls from the country whose ideas of modesty perhaps differ." The solicitor must surely have scorched the sensitivities of young women on remote farms in the Eden Valley!

Pickpockets and "drunks" were among the others who besmirched the Whitsuntide and Martinmas fairs.

The "shows" often included menageries, such as that of Buffalo Bill in 1899. This hit the headlines when Ali Camanza, Maryland, Baltimore, USA, a lion tamer, was attacked by a six-year-old lion which tore his right arm below the elbow. A medical man, Dr Thomson, dashed to the scene to dress the wound and the tamer went on with his performances.

Hiring fairs once took place at Carlisle, Kendal, Cockermouth, Appleby and Kirkby Stephen, as well as Penrith. They were always reported in the local papers, with details of how much servants, male and female, young and old, were to be paid for the next term or half-year. The Carlisle hirings generally took place in Lowther Street, while at Appleby farmers and men congregated around Low Cross to make their deals.

At Penrith the large square known as Sandgate was the gathering ground on hiring days, but activity was later transferred to nearby Burrowgate. Girls and farmhouse women, in presenting themselves for hire, stood alongside men in the street until this was considered unseemly and a hiring room for female servants was set up in a church hall. The *Herald* report of the Whitsuntide hirings in 1914 contained this paragraph:

"The St Andrew's parish rooms were again placed at the disposal of the women but there was a remarkable scarcity. Up to noon Miss Wright and Miss Brooks, Penrith, who had charge of the hiring room, reported that, though there were over 30 applications for women and girl servants, only six parties came to terms, so limited was the supply of labour."

The wages being paid for the half-year at Penrith in 1914 were summarised as follows: Best men, £18-£22; second men, £16-£18; strong youths, £11-£15; best women, £11½-£15; young women, £10-£11; girls, £7-£10. "Bargains made were decidedly in favour of the servants," according to a press report.

The quality and quantity of farmhouse food could be a key factor in determining whether a worker took up the offer of a job. If the farmer's dog appeared to be well-fed, the labourer generally accepted; if the canine had a lean and hungry look, he might well decide to seek other offers!

The landing of a new job was often celebrated in one of the pubs, which did brisk business on hiring days. At Penrith there were attempts to counter the threat of over-indulgence in alcohol. The temperance movement announced in a newspaper advertisement that the large hall at Exchange Buildings, in Angel Lane, would be

A general view of the hustle and bustle of Appleby New Fair, a great Eden Valley gathering. *(Frederick C. Wilson)*

set apart for supplying tea and other non-alcoholic refreshments to farm servants and other visitors. The buildings, later the clothing shop of J.H. Howe, were demolished during the 1980s to make way for the Angel Square shopping mall. Exchange Lane, leading from Angel Lane to Angel Square, marks the former site.

The introduction of district wages committees improved conditions for farm workers, although there was still haggling over money at the fairs. At Penrith, in 1925, best men secured from £35 to £38 for the half-year, second men £25 to £30, youths £16 to £22, boys £11 to £16 and women up to £32 (there being a scarcity of female labour).

Economic factors caused farmers' priorities to vary. During the inter-war years, when money was tight, many of them felt that a lad of 19 or 20 was a better proposition than an older worker who was entitled to the full adult labourer's rate of pay.

The last pre-war hirings were in 1939, but at Penrith very little business was done, as the *Herald* reported: "To find a farmer at Penrith hirings on Tuesday who had succeeded in engaging a farm man was like searching for the proverbial needle in a haystack. Or, to use a literary allusion, he was as elusive as the Scarlet Pimpernel ... There were hirings, as established by custom, and there were scores of people in Burrowgate, but there was no hiring. At least, if there was, it was difficult to discover."

Newspaper advertising – "man or strong youth wanted for tractor or farm work" – was killing off the hiring fairs, but there can have been few regrets. Farm workers were less bucolic than in former years and, quite rightly, they resented having to stand in the streets to be eyed and questioned, on display, rather like tups at an agricultural show.

The hirings survived for a few years after the 1939-45 war. Although few engagements were made, the day was still recognised as a holiday and workers seized the opportunity to visit town for a few drinks or call at the barber's shop. For some, it would be the first proper haircut for six months, for since their last trip into town they had kept each other tidy with pudding basins over heads in farm kitchens.

Few people can have mourned the passing of the old hiring fairs. Traditional they might have been, and picturesque in a rowdy sort of way, but they were lacking in dignity and had a tinge of the slave market.

The fairground element was both more acceptable and more spectacular and the hurdy-gurdy music blared out in Penrith's Great Dockray long after the demise of the hirings. There was genuine regret in town when, by order of the urban council, "the shows" were removed from the central site to an out-of-the-way car park where, somehow, the old appeal was lacking.

Farmers still seek labour from time to time. Nowadays, however, they don't advertise for experienced workers and strong lads but for professional herdspersons and herd managers with skills in dealing with cattle, sheep, pigs, poultry and even llamas.

12

Truly rural ...

Turning off the tortuous A66 road at Sandford, between Appleby and Brough, can be equated to escaping from hell and discovering paradise – getting away from the clamour and threat and finding tranquillity. The trunk road is one of the most hectic in the north of England, bedevilled by an appalling accident record.

Only a mile or so away from the Sandford turn-off is Warcop, a quiet and picturesque Eden Valley village, enriched with bird song, a babbling brook, delightful vistas – and Gregson's shop.

Few village shops have survived the spread of supermarkets in bigger centres but the Warcop store is still going strong after 170 years. Throughout that time six generations of the Gregson family have been supplying the community with groceries and other essentials.

One of the hubs of local life, a busy and vibrant place, the shop is under the control of Michael Gregson, a man who can talk about any aspect of life in Warcop and district and, in particular, about the shop.

It was in 1829 that the Gregson association with the shop began, following the marriage of Mary Gregson to Robert Atkinson, a grocer and draper. On his death, Mary carried on the business until a nephew, Richard Gregson, was old enough to join her. He later bought the shop and took over completely and, since his tenure, in the mid-1800s, there have been four further generations.

Around 1880, brothers John Richardson and Thomas Brass followed their father, Richard, trading as grocers and butter factors. Next came John Richard and Thomas, better known by their nicknames of "Bundy" and "Blam", who ran the shop until the 1950s when the business passed to the present incumbent, Michael. His son, David, represents the sixth generation of the family to sell Warcop folk their butter, sugar and tea, although he also runs a family shop in the nearby town of Kirkby Stephen.

Michael's reminiscences include stories of his earliest involvement – as an errand boy, making deliveries on a bicycle, with a wicker basket on the handlebars. Those were the days of wooden counters, massive rounds of cheese, spectacular sides of home-cured ham, vinegar in wooden barrels, and brass scales for the weighing out of sugar, lard, bacon, dried fruit and biscuits.

Another piece of equipment was a butter worker, which was operated by hand. The butter, brought in from local farms, was made up into pounds, either for sale over the counters or for dispatch by train to Bradford and other bigger places. Out went the old wooden counters in 1974 when the shop was converted to self-service in a link-up with the Spar organisation. Seeing the place for the first time with new metal shelving installed, a veteran customer commented: "I don't know whether to laugh or cry."

As well as being Warcop's grocer, Michael Gregson is its historian and in the room above the shop are his many records – postcards, bulging scrapbooks of newspaper cuttings, old minute books and reminders of old-established events like the village rushbearing, a colourful annual festival.

There is also a short poem penned by a customer:

> Please put the bacon and eggs on.
> Run out? Then ring up Gregson,
> Or, better, pay him a call.
> You'll find he will furnish all
> Your wants for a day or week.
> His stock is quite unique.

Nothing is perfect. But village life, long ago, came very close to my impressions of Utopia.

Under the placid surface, there could be rifts and back-biting, disruptive householders and declines in community spirit. The parish council of an Eden Valley village received a request for help from a newcomer to the neighbourhood in trying to persuade a farmer to re-route his cows, on their way for milking, so that there would be no mess on the roadway outside her house. Some chance!

So life in the countryside has its occasional turmoils but embedded deep in my memory are golden flashes of village life in childhood days:

Water jetting noisily into buckets from squeaky, hand-operated pumps ... the ting of the door-bell and the chatter of customers, on entering the village shop ... young men, with caps turned back to front, sitting astride motorbikes on street corners ... feeding hens, calling out "Chuck, chuck, chuck" ... the delicious smell of home-baked bread ... small boys getting a pre-match ride on the cricket roller ... crossing a cobbled yard to the two-seater earth closet ... the rare thrill of seeing an aeroplane overhead ... grand-motherly advice to "Wrap up warm" ... the notice board with its tat-tered, wind-blown messages telling of dances, whist drives, parish council meetings and 'coming attractions' at the cinema in the near-est town ... Monday morning washlines, some with undergarments chastely masked by billowing bedsheets, others with fulsome knickers fluttering blatantly ...

These are some of the delights recalled by indulging in a little nostalgia of a wonderfully laid-back era, a time of tranquil content-ment, when villages were virtually isolated, with few cars and buses going into town and that only once or twice a week.

So there was heavy dependence upon on-the-spot skills, ser-vices, initiatives and individuals. Individuals like the village bobby who pounded beats in rural lanes, checked doors at midnight, kept a watchful eye on children as they crossed the road on leaving school, and supervised sheep-dipping in farm fields.

There was an agreeable sense of security when communities had resident local policemen. They were not temporary characters in those days, anxious to get away to a posting with more potential for advancement, but men who were happy with their lifestyles, involved in local activities and with children in good hands at a nearby school.

PC Stanley Mason spent 26 years as bobby at Plumpton, on the A6, a few miles north of Penrith. He was much more than the repre-sentative of law and order, and a key figure in local life. In the 1920s

Children at play outside the village school at Crosby Garrett in Upper Eden – one of the many country schools to be closed during the 1970s, despite much local campaigning.

he travelled into Scotland to buy a redundant building which was transported to Plumpton and transformed into the village hall. Then, Stanley Mason virtually ran the place, as honorary secretary. "He was a good policeman and a good friend," said one speaker at a farewell ceremony when he left in 1947. Nearly 250 people contributed to a cash presentation and everybody sang "Auld Lang Syne" as PC and Mrs. Mason departed.

The village copper tackled local crimes single-handed. Some of them were far from being sensational but they could disrupt local life. A gang of youngsters toured the district around the village of Skelton, opening field gates, so that cattle strayed in numbers; farmers were irate and protested vociferously to the new bobby, David Fallowfield. Inquiries in pubs led him to four suspects and, although they fiercely denied causing the trouble, the policeman issued strong warnings – a result which convinced the farming community that "summat" had been done in response to their complaints.

Boys at play at Morland, a pretty village which lies in the valley of the Lyvennet, one of the Eden's tributaries. *(John T. Hall)*

Like Stanley Mason, many years earlier, David Fallowfield was accepted as a villager in the fullest sense, a member of committees and chairman of the silver jubilee committee in 1977.

Pods of peas were pilfered from the school garden at Wreay, near Carlisle. PC Brian Thompson kept a late-night watch and surprised two teenagers as they helped themselves to more. A stern talking-to sufficed; next morning the boys turned up at the school to apologise. We no longer have resident policemen who, among their more official duties, might find the time to cut the lawn of an elderly woman or chop logs for another. It was a caring role; just how caring depended on the individual.

The weekly or fortnightly 'gathering grounds' for rural police officers were the country courthouses where they turned up in numbers to prove cases of farmers whose sheep strayed on to roads, owners of dogs without licences, learner-motorists without L-plates, cyclists without lights or who rode "two on a bike". Lunch-breaks provided the opportunity for a spot of conversational socialising. The courthouse in the village of Hackthorpe, on the A6, was ideally situated alongside the pub, the Lowther Castle (of which it is now part).

The genteel landlady, Mrs. Graham, put on two types of meal for the court attenders. In the front room, the JPs, solicitors, court officials and others of quality sat down to neat, crustless sandwiches and coffee from the best cups. Police officers, reporters, witnesses and, sometimes, defendants shared a less dignified room at the back of the premises – but the sandwiches were more generous and the prices lower.

On-the-spot policing was clearly favoured by a one-time chief constable. The issue of more motorcycles to village bobbies was urged during the 1950s, but he resisted the move, saying that his officers would see far more from the saddles of pushbikes!

Economies of the 1980s put an end to the era of country coppers who were replaced by a mobile force, moving by van from village to village. A senior officer tried to justify the change by describing the effectiveness of the old-timers as "a myth". Communities lost hands-on guardianship when officers were diverted from the countryside to deal with national problems which had not previously loomed so large – drugs, football hooliganism and travelling criminals who sped up and down the motorways.

Gone, alas, were the days when Dick Little, at Temple Sowerby, Tommy Hood, at Cliburn, or Stanley Mason, at Plumpton, pedalled their pushbikes or rode their motorcycles along rural lanes, hoping for the chance for a chat beside a farm gate or outside a village shop. They brought a feeling of security and well-being to folk who lived in remote spots because they were just a mile or two, or a phone call away. That was no myth.

Not only departing and retiring policemen received gifts from grateful residents. They also showed their appreciation of those other characters of a past era, local postmen who covered vast distances on foot and on pedal cycles. Walter Jackson retired in 1947 after 28 years' service as postman at Matterdale, near Ullswater, and was handed a pipe, a pouch, lighter and a voucher for 28 ounces of baccy. Letters to local newspapers were other marks of appreciation. After the blizzards of 1947, a resident of Dacre wrote: "Our particular postman, Mr H. Donnison, fought his way through snow and drifts on days when it was not fit to be outside and he was forced to walk the many miles per day, as riding a bicycle was impossible."

This prompted another tribute, from Temple Sowerby: "During those five weeks of severe weather our 'postie' trudged over fields and hedges, calling at farms and cottages and covering about 15 miles each day ... The bus failed us for ten days but not once the mails."

When indomitable country postmen called it a day, there were sometimes estimates of how far they had walked – the equivalent of having been round the world on foot, in some cases. Tom Webster, the Great Strickland 'postie', who estimated that he walked and cycled 269,000 miles in his 47-year stint, said that the job also had its compensations – the cups of tea and other hospitality, received from folk along the route, which helped to sustain him.

The chumminess of rural life in its heyday emerged when a policeman or a postman retired or moved on. Thomas Thompson (or "Tommy Postie"), long-service postman at Calthwaite up to 1972, was reported to have been a voluntary carrier of news of stray sheep, deliverer of turnip seed and adviser to farmers on when the local thresher was due to visit them. He collected pensions, swept away the snow and got in the coals for elderly residents, making him well worthy of the occasional reward of a package of sausage and black pudding. It was said that Tommy's favourite sound was that of a pig squealing!

A one-time Bishop of Carlisle, the Right Rev. Cyril Bulley, used to say that the requirements of churchwardens, in seeking a new parish priest, were so demanding that only the Archangel Gabriel would have sufficed and, as he was not available, they had to make do with the next best thing. Church of England parsons and ministers of other religious persuasions, once a familiar sight as they chatted with parishioners in villages of any size, have diminished in numbers, as a result of cost-cutting exercises and mergers. Clergymen now tend to serve groups of neighbourhood churches, either individually or in teams.

The vicars of old did not limit their activities to preaching sermons and supping cups of tea with old ladies. Canon Tom Baily, the Shap vicar, loved sport and, in an unobtrusive way, helped to make his village the sporting stronghold that it was. He was timekeeper and judge at sports meetings, served as scorer for the cricket team and followed the football teams of all age groups. If one of them happened to lift a trophy there was always a champagne celebration in the dressing room, with the vicar providing the bottles. Richard Porthouse, a Penrith cricket lover, summed up a perfect summer day: "The sun's shining out of a cloudless sky, there's a Conservative Government in power and Canon Baily is scoring on the cricket field, wearing his MCC tie."

The Rev. Charles Barrand had one of the tiniest parishes of England. Far-flung Martindale, nestling alongside Ullswater, in the Northern Lakes, had only 80 parishioners during his time there – but there were two churches to maintain, the historic St Martin's, built about 1630, and the more modern St Peter's.

Back in 1877, a Bishop of Carlisle had difficulty in finding a parson for Martindale and commented: "The position of the parish, in a secluded mountain glen, is so peculiar that it is not every clergyman who is suited to it." The remoteness did not deter Charles Barrand who moved to Martindale from Blackpool in 1963, and described the experience as "From the Golden Mile to country style". He became one of Ullswater's leading publicists by means of his novel money-making venture of publishing picture postcards and Christmas cards, showing scenes in the dale, and sold thousands through local shops to boost funds and publicise his two churches, with the result that in one year thousands of people visited ancient St Martin's.

Charles Barrand, a man of enterprise and energy, loved Martindale, of which he once said: "Every day it shows a different face as the seasons change. The storm clouds gather round, and the winds tear down the dales, and the picture is one of frightening grandeur. Yet, with a haze of heat hanging over the valleys, and seen from the mountain tops, this might be some Shangri-La where all is still and quiet, filled with peace for evermore."

One of the most colourful characters in the post-war history of Appleby was the town's vicar throughout the 1960s, the Rev. Geoffrey Dixon. As a councillor he was something of a "stormy petrel" and at one stage startled the town and the town council by resigning his position as Mayor's chaplain and saying that he would take no part in council affairs until he received an assurance from the Minister of Local Government that he was satisfied with the way in which the authority was conducting its affairs. Regardless of the problems which prompted such a declaration, he continued in local government, became an alderman and then mayor.

Loss of village schools with rolls of under 20 was regrettable enough in itself, but communities also suffered because the teachers, forced to move elsewhere as a result of the closures, were invariably among the trend-setters, sometimes workaholics, who made big contributions to the public life. Impassioned pleas were made in bids to retain small schools, even where the attendance figure had dropped as low as a dozen, as was the case in the village of Crosby Garrett in the 1970s. The local county councillor, Raven Frankland, declared: "If these schools are closed, the villages will become a collection of weekend cottages, the community will fall to pieces and the agriculture will decline."

Alas, his words were all to no effect.

There was something distinctly cherubic about Douglas Thornton, the small, cherry-faced man who became headmaster at Bampton in 1918 and found life so congenial among the folk of the remote Lakeland dale that he remained there for 33 years, despite the urgings of successive directors of education who suggested richer rewards elsewhere. "Duggie" Thornton was one of those cheerful characters who always seemed pleased to see you. He made the place tick through his involvements, including council work and the village sports. He used to recall that when he went to Bampton in 1918 there was only one car in the valley and horse-drawn transport into Penrith only on Tuesdays.

Another livewire of the same era, a man with many public roles, was Frank William Parrott who, on retiring from the headship of the Kirkby Stephen primary school, probably worked even harder as parish, district and county councillor and still found time to report town events for the weekly newspaper.

Village festivals frequently depended on the leadership of the school heads, such as Matthew Pace in promoting the May Day at Lazonby and Miss Harding, who had a similar role at Melmerby. These were not school-related duties, although pupils played a big part in the events, of course.

Not all the villages had doctors resident in the parish but some did. Patterdale, at the southern end of Ullswater was doubly fortunate in the 1960s in having a doctor who was also a considerable leader. In fact, Dr. James D. Ogilvie, or "Doc" Ogilvie, recognised that, with increasing numbers of people roaming the Ullswater fells, an organised rescue service was needed. He was a pioneer and first leader of the Patterdale mountain rescue team, which quickly became one of the busiest in the Lake District. Public service comes neither tougher nor more risky than in mountain rescue work. All the members are volunteers, prepared to leave their beds or firesides, in the middle of the night, and in the worst of weather, to go to the aid of the lost and injured. Moreover, there is so little cash aid for this vital work that the teams have to organise their own events to provide vehicles and other equipment.

Dr. Ogilvie was a climber as well as a rescue leader. While rock climbing in 1967 he fell 60ft., fracturing his skull. As the rescue team from the Ullswater Outward Bound School climbed towards the scene of the mishap, a garbled message came back to the effect that "Doc" Ogilvie was there. Misunderstanding the situation, one of the team said, "Thank God – but how did he get there first this time?"

Although at the other end of the social scale from the doctor or the village schoolmaster, tramps were not as unwelcome as some might now imagine. These homeless men wandered about the countryside, sometimes sleeping rough, sometimes staying in workhouses where they performed small tasks in return for bed and breakfast. If a tramp knocked at the door, seeking hot water in order to brew a can of tea, there were seldom any fears that he would cause trouble or damage. They were generally accepted as benign men who were down on their luck – old soldiers, perhaps – and they might well be given a few coppers or a slice of bread and butter to accompany the tea. Kindly women might give a tramp an old or unwanted item of clothing.

Small-town itinerants tended to be seen as "characters" because of their unusual ways and attire. A middle-aged Penrith man, known mainly by his nickname of "Jellybags", slept rough and made his way about the town, looking for small jobs, always wearing a battered pair of wellington boots. He was never seen in any other kind of footwear, winter or summer, rain or shine. He was not resented when he went for coffee and a snack in Dayson's milkbar but was always given the same cup, plate, knife and fork. Possibly

A happy wanderer. An old-time tramp makes a brew of tea behind a Cumbrian wall. It is many years since such men walked about the Eden countryside, earning themselves a few coppers, a slab of cake or an unwanted item of clothing by doing an odd job. *(Alec Fraser)*

Safe from the lion's den! A Penrith character of yesteryear, Kit ("Jellybags") Wilson went into the lion's cage, by way of a publicity stunt at a circus visiting Penrith in the 1960s.

the only claim to fame of "Jellybags" stemmed from the visit to town by a circus company. By way of a publicity stunt, he agreed to enter the lion's cage on the first night, and his picture duly appeared in the local papers.

Some wandering men visited Cumbrian villages where they offered their services as sharpeners of household knives and hoers of turnips for farmers. Jock Macmillan, a harmless old man who made a precarious living in this way, lived in a quarry near Kings Meaburn until he was found unconscious and died in hospital a few days later. Poor old Jock caused more trouble in death than he did throughout his hermit-like existence, for who was to pay for his funeral? He rests in peace in the churchyard at Morland because the former North Westmorland rural council settled the undertaker's bill.

Technology now rules. Simple background noises like the solemn tick-tock of the corner clock and the friendly crackle of a coal-fire are rarely heard. Just as they have vanished, so have many of the ever-reliable characters who once bestrode the rural scene.

13

"Good tekkin"

The gingerbread made by my grandmother, Sarah Ann Hurst, baked in the oven alongside the coalfire in her little house at Abbeytown in the 1930s, was distinctly different from ordinary gingerbreads, with a flavour and consistency which nobody else could match. In my pursuit of tastiness, hunks of cheese and wedges of ham, surreptitiously sliced from supplies in the village shop of my other grandmother, Isabella Little, were other delicious morsels which I still remember with relish from my childhood days.

If the way to a man's heart is through his stomach, my grannies were among my first girlfriends!

In the days before cake mixes and easy-to-prepare dinners in tinfoil, requiring only a few minutes of heating-up, home cooking ruled. Meals out were a rarity; so were visits to fish and chip shops. Holidays abroad to sample Continental dishes and French wines were not even in our wildest dreams.

Family meals tended to follow a weekly pattern. After roast beef on Sunday, there was invariably sliced cold meat on Monday and shepherds' pie on the dinner table on Tuesday, as the remnants of the roast could be minced up to provide the meaty content of the pie.

In a county with more sheep than men, dishes containing mutton were frequently on the menu. Tatie-pot, a luscious mixture of the meat of the Herdwick sheep, with potatoes, carrots, onions and black pudding, all sloshing in gravy, was a regular treat in Lakeland households. Its fame spread far beyond the county boundaries, for the delicate flavour of Herdwick mutton graced the

The shop in King Street, Penrith, where the now-famous Penrith toffee and fudge were first made my Mrs Annie Furnass, using a secret recipe. Her customers included members of the Royal family. The sweetmeats are no longer produced and sold in King Street and the shop now sells second-hand clothes.

banqueting tables at Buckingham Palace. A farmers' meeting was once told that on the menus of posh hotels in Paris was "Paté de pomme de terre Herdwick" – a French version of our tatie-pot.

Much sausage masquerades as the Cumberland variety. Generally, the genuine 'Cumberland' is thicker, meatier and in distinctive coils, a world apart in tastiness from the blander copy-cat types. Originally, it took its name from the Cumberland pig, once a breed in its own right, as well known as the Tamworth or the Large White. Its unique flavour was extolled by R. W. Bell, a one-time secretary of the NFU in Cumberland and North Westmorland: "We fear no comparison with the peach-fed pigs of the depraved New World. In Cumberland we appreciate our own cure. We scorn such fussy words as 'succulent' to describe so rare a flavour; we are well content with the description 'fine', or should we say 'finest'?"

The Cumberland pig, as a breed, faded out many years ago, mainly because the ham it produced was thought to be too fatty. Happily, Cumberland sausage lives on, obviously not exactly according to the original recipe – but still a prince among sausages.

What a lovely laugh! Royal mirth marked a visit to the Penrith headquarters of Eden District Council in 1991, centered on the presentation to the Queen of a box of Penrith fudge or toffee by council chairman Mac Carlyle. Photographer Fred Wilson captured the magical moment. *(Frederick C. Wilson)*

To really appreciate Cumbrian culinary skills, I recommend a close-up vision of one of the country shows. Alluring aromas drift from marquees, full of exhibits on long trestle tables. Earnest women move about the big tents, pausing from time to time to pass judgement on appetising rows of rhubarb pies, rum butter and raspberry sponges, queues of crusty loaves, custard tarts and currant cakes, line-ups of lemon meringue pies and luscious lunch-time titbits. A joy for any trencherman to behold – but, sadly, he must not touch or taste.

A newspaper report of the cookery section of Hesket Newmarket show in the late-1940s included this paragraph: "Just think of it – 30 sandwich cakes all in a row. And other classes not far behind in numbers. As one person remarked, 'It was turble thrang int' tent'."

The highlight of any agricultural show was (and is) the luncheon, consisting of big helpings of meat salad, accompanied by pickles, sliced beetroot, tea, bread and butter, and followed by trifle or fruit salad, with ice-cream. Show lunches must never be gobbled. The occasion is one to relish and linger over, while enjoying the "crack", and, in some cases, to drink toasts to the show society and those essential people, the judges of livestock, crafts and foodstuffs.

The tendency to think of villages, rather than towns, as bastions of fine cooking and scrumptious food is probably due to the influence of the Women's Institutes who, if not listening to talks about preparing perfect picnics or Christmas treats, hold competitions for hot cross buns, jams, scones or biscuits. There is a lighter side to the WI contests when members display such rare skills as peeling potatoes when blindfold and eating jelly or peas with knitting needles.

Tips on keeping husbands happy have sometimes featured in the WI competitions, a theme also touched upon by the compilers of the Dufton and Knock parish church cookery book, published in 1948.

"Face powder may get you a man – but it takes baking powder to keep him," one woman advised. Another contributed a brief verse:

> "We may live without friends,
> We may live without books.
> But civilised men
> Cannot live without cooks"

As though to underline the point, there was a dialect poem in praise of local womenfolk, written by Harold Deighton:

> "Thoo mun git a lass frae Dufton
> An' deah as weel as me.
> She'll mak o'soarts o'stuff ta eat,
> Like berry keaak fer tea.
> Apple dumplings an' reubarb tarts,
> Yearb puddin', pez puddin an' sek
> Wi' treacle taffy an' brandy snaps,
> An' hyam-meade wines ta lep."

The "yearb puddin", referred to by the poet, translates into herb pudding with nettles and dandelion leaves. Or you might prefer poacher's pie ("first clean and joint your rabbit") or sheep's head broth ("take one sheep's head, soak overnight in salt and water, scrape well and put on with sufficient water to cover ... ").

Some of the other recipes in Cumbrian cookbooks have more to do with personal happiness than delicious dishes, but are still worthy of record. A WI 'dish for lovers' goes like this: "1 little duck, 1 nice young man, 2 sweet hearts, 2 kindred souls, 1 shady nook.

Squeeze well together, first removing all prying eyes; add a few small nothings and sifted moonlight; flavour with kisses, onions not required; serve as required."

If in less romantic mood, there are personal qualities which can give a sparkle to daily life, as in the verse:

"Take one whole pound of kindliness
And stir it round with thoughts that bless.
Plenty of patience makes it nice,
Some fun will add a pleasant spice.
Don't weigh out love but pour it in,
Oil of good cheer will grease your tin,
Mix well in just the same old-time way,
And you'll have made a special day."

Thoughts of food in days long past automatically spark thoughts of village shops of special memory, friendly places full of mouth-watering smells. These were the chatty centres of togetherness; shopkeepers issued news and tittle-tattle with the tea, flour, butter, eggs, tinned fruit and all the rest. In one of these small shops, run by a very dear relative, the smell of bread baking wafted through from the kitchen; the crust of a fresh loaf, just out of the oven and with a blob of butter melting on it, was a meal fit for a king. Such shops now struggle to survive; many have already submitted to the supermarkets.

Even Cumbria, so rich in renown for its old-time tastiness and traditional dishes, could not escape the invasion of foreign fare, from China, Italy, India, Spain and other countries. The trend started in Penrith many years ago when Lizzie Eland's little fish and chip shop, in Langton Street, was renamed the "Lotus Garden", under new management. Among other changes, an old pub, the Greyhound, gave way to an Indian restaurant, under the alluring title of "Taste of Bengal", while Taylor's cafe, where fish, chips and mushy peas once went down a treat, took on a trendier atmosphere when it became the "Golden City" chop suey house.

The Queen's visit to Penrith in 1991, as part of a short tour of Cumbria, produced a moment to cherish in revealing a royal sweet tooth. A stunning picture of Her Majesty by Fred Wilson, a Penrith news photographer, captured a brief interlude of unrestrained mirth and happiness, a lovely laugh, as she received a two-pound box of Penrith's famous fudge from the chairman of Eden District

Steaming hot tatie pot — the ideal fare on a chilly day. This picture, from 1977, shows women of Caldbeck preparing dinner at an event in honour of huntsman John Peel.

Council, Mac Carlyle. It emerged that the Penrith Toffee Shop regularly despatched boxes of the mouth-watering fudge to Buckingham Palace, although it was addressed to one of HM pages. Was it the revelation of her sweet secret which caused the gusts of laughter from the Queen and the Duke of Edinburgh? Whatever the reason, it was a lovely laugh.

The originator of Penrith toffee and fudge, Mrs. Annie Furnass, became known to thousands of customers, some in distant parts of the country. Her husband, William, had a butcher's shop in the town's King Street and she opened a sweet shop nearby. It was after William died in 1924 that she concentrated on her own business, starting to make toffee from a secret recipe. Penrith toffee and fudge achieved phenomenal success and Annie Furnass had some distinguished patrons, including the Duke of Kent, who once called on her when motoring through town. The product passed out of the Furnass family's ownership, but is still made in town and is still a

Just like mother used to bake them! Mrs Mary Stuart, of Threlkeld WI, casts an experienced eye over the fruit cakes on show at Mungrisdale. *(J.M. Brookes)*

favourite of famous folk. Still on sweet things, Penrith is the cream cake "capital" of Cumbria through being the long-time headquarters of J.R. Birkett and Sons Ltd., whose coffee puffs, eclairs and cream sponges are sold in all parts of the county and beyond.

Kennedy's Fine Chocolates, made in the old school at Orton, travel the world because they are given in sachets to people setting out on long air flights. One of the newer flavours of the county is that of Cumberland honey mustard, a product of the Pennine town of Alston since 1983. Honey, nutmeg and mustard seed, mixed in Alston spring water, with salt to taste, give a versatile substance which is more wide-ranging than ordinary mustard; some people prefer to spread it on toast or use it to pep up their cheese or ham sandwiches.

For an impression of the robustness of the Cumbrian appetite, consider a case heard before a County Court in the late-1940s, which centred on the feeding of men working on a farm in the course of a typical day:

Breakfast: Porridge, with new milk (sometimes syrup), a slice of home-cured bacon and tea ... **10 o'clocks:** "Drinkings", with bread, cheese and gingerbread ... **Mid-day:** Two plates of meat and potatoes, two plates of milk pudding ... **4 o'clock:** Three or four slices of bread and jam, home-made pasty and cake ... **Supper:** Always a "knife and fork" meal, varying in content from day to day.

Surely, there must have been enough nutrition in such a daily intake – but not for one lusty lad of 17. He left his farm job prematurely, complaining that he was under-fed, as he was refused second helpings. When he appeared in court, on a charge of a breach of contract, a surprised solicitor commented, "I sometimes feel tempted to change places with the farmers." Judge Allsebrook understood his feelings. "I don't blame you if it is food you are talking about," he said.

Yet the case of the hungry farm lad is no means unique, for some Cumbrian appetites can be quite staggering in the quantity of rich food which can be demolished at a single sitting. A party of Penrith sportsmen called at a roadside cafe, the Astra, near High Hesket, on the A6, around 1960. The order was for mixed grills – ham and eggs, with chips, peas, tomatoes, mushrooms, fried bread – a mini-mountain of food for each consumer when the plates were carried through from the kitchen.

Except in the case of one solid citizen, a miner. He asked for double helpings of the lot – and didn't leave a scrap.

No doubt the feast was "good tekkin". Hear those words in the Eden Valley and you know that a tasty meal has been eaten with relish.

14

Glory of Eden

Modernity, in its many forms, is alarmingly irrepress-ible, thrusting its way into old landscapes and changing long-established lifestyles. Heavyweight containers and other speeding traffic on motorways, like the M6 through Cumbria, contrast sharply with the easy-going ways of yesteryear. Progress is not always prettifying.

Thankfully, there is still time and encouragement to stop and stare in more sublime areas like the Eden Valley of Cumbria. There are still unspoilt landscapes which big city developers have not found ... still patches of breathtaking colour ... still a few shops of character like that of Arnisons the drapers, in the middle of Penrith, where customers step back in time in purchasing for the future, and the head of the firm, Deryck Scott, knows almost everybody, their relatives and most personal details.

Although Cumbria is thought of as a county of rugged mountains and plunging valleys, prone to harsh weather in the depths of winter, it also has the haunting beauty of the unsung Eden Valley, in its many moods.

The captivation of the valley, with its surrounding countryside in northern Lakeland and the Pennine slopes, first struck me over 40 years ago on a sunlit visit to South Stainmore. Looking down the valley, it was as though a vast, multi-coloured carpet, rather irregu-lar because of undulations in the land, stretched ahead of me towards the distant fells of the Lake District.

After that glorious initiation, I found much more to relish in the richness of the landscape. Early-morning is the best time to refresh the soul by taking in one of the vistas. Perhaps the stillness of

Ullswater, as seen through the trees in the descent from Gowbarrow Fell ... the view from Penrith Beacon Edge as the mist lingers over the lower land towards Stainton and Tirril, giving it an ethereal quality ... or the awakening of hidden-away villages like Newby, Sleagill, Maulds Meaburn, Great Asby and Crosby Garrett as the first smoke curls from the chimney pots and the dew gives an added gloss to the hedgerows.

Midsummer in Upper Eden is a time of floral delights. Amidst the spectacular patchwork of narrow roads, wooded areas, streams and fields – some of the best farming land in England – there are radiant days of rustic

The Gregson family have run the village shop at Warcop, in the Eden Valley, for over 170 years. Now in charge are Michael and Valerie, with son David (right). *(Frederick C. Wilson)*

pleasure in the neighbouring villages of Warcop and Great Musgrave, which both stage festivals in which flowers play a part.

Schoolgirls bind blooms into crowns, which they wear in processions to the parish churches, while boys carry crosses of rushes. The rushbearings, as they are known, are a present-day re-enactment of a simple medieval ritual, the annual renewal of the rushes which covered church floors. They are gentle, leisurely occasions, with brass bands playing, sunshine gleaming through overhanging trees and proud parents relishing the sight of children in their "Sunday best" reliving a fragment of local history, amidst lush scenery.

One of the oldest of the traditional events of the Eden Valley is the annual rushbearing in the village of Warcop. Girls wearing floral crowns and boys carrying crosses of rushes walk in procession to the parish church. *(Frederick C Wilson)*

There was a time when rushbearing day ended in sports, generally a mixture of races for village youngsters and visiting athletes competing for cash prizes. Organisers are less ambitious these days and evening activities may well be limited to a domino drive.

Further down the valley, the May days at Langwathby and Melmerby, on spacious village greens, are also floral festivals. In days gone by, the Melmerby Queen wore a crown of forget-me-nots and a garland of red geraniums, white rock, lilies and maidenhair, and she pronounced:

> Brighter far than gold or gem,
> I this flowery diadem
> Wear upon my brow today,
> That shall crown your Queen of May.

Although the picturesque ceremony is a yearly milestone of village life, there is an underlying message of respect for wildlife. The

May Queen's proclamation once read: "To all her beloved subjects, the Queen commands that they shall be kind to all animals – that they shall not hunt the wrens, or stone the squirrels, or chase the cats, or rob birds' nests; but shall learn by heart the notes of birds, and know when they come and when they go, and how they sing and what they say; that they shall not kill or hurt any living thing needlessly, or destroy any beautiful thing, but shall strive to save all gentle life; that they shall not root up ferns, nor break down blossoming trees, but shall learn the names of the flowers and their seasons and habits, and watch the budding of the trees."

The floral glory of Eden is deep-rooted in a simple pride in the appearance of gardens and cottage-fronts. Enthusiasts are catered for by garden centres, full of seeds, bulbs, plants and other essentials, which have sprung up, one of them in the former village railway station at Culgaith.

Pride is strongest in communities whose parish councils have given a lead, over many years, and householders, children, farmers and publicans have collaborated in an annual best-kept village competition, initially run by the Cumberland Council of Social Services. Although Voluntary Action Cumbria took over and altered the name to "Cumbria in bloom", the contest is still aimed at keeping villages both tidy and appealing, and flowers play a big part.

The historic village of Kirkoswald won the contest in the first year of 1958. While the judges were impressed by the absence of litter and the tidiness of bus shelters, 'phone boxes and notice boards, the masses of flowers also took the eye.

A journalist on the *Herald* wrote: "There are flowers in every available nook and cranny. There are flowers in hanging baskets, window troughs and stone urns, tiny beds and narrow borders. Women householders have produced a riot of colour with a floral display of remarkable variety. Kirkoswald seems to make a feature of roses, for which this has been a vintage year, and the judges just happened to pay a visit when the roses were at their best."

In the days before Dr. Beeching's axe fell on rural railway lines, the appearance of village stations was also a cause of pride. Stationmasters and porters devoted countless hours to rose beds and flower borders in the hope of winning one of the BR awards.

The village of Dufton, at the foot of the Pennines, is built around the green, which was once the setting for the annual agricultural show, known as the "Fellside Royal".
(John T. Hall)

Cumbria's lady of flowers in the 1970s and 1980s was the late Mrs. Sylvia Mary McCosh, a member of the Hasell family of Dalemain, between Penrith and Ullswater, whose articles in the *Herald* were likened to "a refreshing breath of cool, country air, delicately scented with the fragrance of roses after rain". She wrote two books, the second of them a selection of the pieces she had written for the newspaper, along with some verses which her love of flowers inspired. A leading horticulturist once chose "Sylvia Mary" and "Dalemain" as the names of new varieties of sweet peas.

Most of the people of the Eden Valley have easy access to field walks, although along the line of the M6 some of them have been curtailed and are not as convenient as they used to be. These rural strolls opened up the floral delights of fields and hedgerows in the times when walking was a cheap and popular homespun pleasure and, in summer, hosts of people took to the fields to hear bird calls, see rabbits and hares scampering, and identify wild flowers which flourished in numbers and varieties. Courting couples were among

"Smile, please . . .". Children of Melmerby, taking part in the annual May Day
ceremony in 1971, seem strangely reluctant to oblige the photographer. Melmerby
and neighbouring Langwathby have held May Days for many years.

the walkers – though the study of flora and fauna may not have been
their prime motive.

Sadly, the motor car reduced the popularity of the country walk,
certainly so far as young couples were concerned. A headline in the
Herald in 1958 read, "Lovers' lanes falling into neglect". Mr. J.
Hartley, chairman of the Cumberland Parish Councils'Association,
said the younger generation were using cars, often travelling great
distances, while courting. They no longer walked the country
paths, along riverbanks and through woodlands where sunshine
flickered through the branches and, as a result, many footpaths and
ancient rights of way were in danger of being lost through neglect.

Because of major changes in cultivation, many old-fashioned
flowers and grasses have disappeared from farmers' fields. However, Cumbria County Council, supported by the county's wildlife
trust, have turned many of its 2,000 miles of roadside verges into

nature reserves. Every stretch of verge is surveyed, and sensible policies are adopted for cutting, so that rare plants are safeguarded. Other highway authorities are less considerate, cutting the roadside grasses before uncommon flowers have formed seeds. The intensification of agricultural methods since the 1939-45 war has removed much variety and colour from the fields but in Cumbria, at least, the verges offer glimpses of past glories.

Local folk have always been aware that the Eden Valley is quite special but it has also received recognition from afar in a proposal by English Nature to make the valley a Site of Special Scientific Interest – of "national, even European importance" because of its unspoilt quality, its wildlife and plant varieties.

The fascination lies not just in flowers and greenery, of course. In villages and in the open countryside the attention of the passer-by may be seized by unusual features. Kings Meaburn, near Appleby, an unpretentious village with a single road running through, boasts road signs topped with crowns to indicate its "royal" status. A notice peeping over a garden wall tells travellers they are in the 'County of Westmorland', ignoring the fact that it became part of Cumbria under local government reorganisation in the 1970s.

Some roadside inns carry poetic pleas on the signs. The Beehive Inn at Eamont Bridge, just south of Penrith – a hostelry which dates back to 1727 – tells travellers on the A6:

> In this hive we're all alive.
> Good liquor makes us funny.
> If you be dry,
> Step in and try the virtue of our honey.

At the nearby Yanwath Gate Inn, between Eamont Bridge and Ullswater, the message on the sign reads:

> This gate hangs well
> And hinders none.
> Refresh and pay
> And travel on.

Medieval stocks are a feature of Gamblesby, at the foot of the Cumbrian Pennines, a village which suffers when the notorious Helm wind strikes. However great a misdemeanour, surely an offender would not be punished there when the wind was at its worst!

Winter casts its lustre on Hutton-in-the-Forest, at a crossroads on the route between Penrith and Wigton. *(Alec Fraser)*

In Stainton, near Penrith, a small housing estate is named "The Pavilion", a reminder of the fact that the village's original cricket field was located there.

Built into a field wall at Plumpton, a village to the north of Penrith, is a memorial to PC Joseph Byrnes, the local bobby, recalling how in October 1885 he was murdered on that spot by burglars when he tackled them single-handed after they had raided Netherby Hall, near Carlisle.

A few miles to the east, alongside the Lazonby to Great Salkeld road, a horse trough, installed in 1902, carries this message for posterity: "Erected to commemorate the Coronation of King Edward VII and also in appreciation of the lessening of the gradients of Scatterbeck Hill by Cumberland County Council. Drink. Thank. Think."

15

Nostalgia in stone

Saturday night was special. If the working week had been full of worries and frustrations, they were temporarily forgotten in a few hours of drinking and dancing, rhythm and romance. For Saturday night was Drill Hall night when all roads – mainly from the public houses – led to the "bob hop" where hundreds jigged to the mellow tones of Frank Walton and the Melody Makers.

The Saturday evening pattern of socialising seldom varied. Unattached young men generally had preliminary get-togethers at one of the milkbars – the Beechwood, in Middlegate, or Dayson's, at the foot of Castlegate – before moving on to one or more of the pubs. The Gloucester Arms was one of the popular ones with the sporty set, while others might frequent the Two Lions, on the other side of Great Dockray, or the Mitre, in King Street. Then, as the 10 o'clock closing time approached in those and other pubs, departing groups converged in Middlegate or Corney Square as they headed towards the Penrith Drill Hall on foot.

Single girls had probably been there for some time, often dancing with each other in the absence of men. Coats were deposited with an elderly couple at the back of the hall before those without partners spent a few minutes "eyeing the talent" – those of the opposite sex who might appreciate their company.

Saturday dance nights were superb value for a shilling – just 5p in today's coinage. Frank Walton was Penrith's Glenn Miller, playing the favourite melodies of the day and occasionally bursting into something much livelier, such as *I've got a lovely bunch of coconuts*.

Penrith pride – the Musgrave Monument clock, in the middle of the town, provided a backcloth for this picture of Col. George Kinmont, a man of military bearing who ran a civic trust scheme to improve the appearance of the town in the 1960s. *(Robert Armstrong)*

Romance was often the motive in the choice of partners, for asking a girl to take the dance floor might well be a prelude to offering to walk her home later in the evening. Among the foxtrots, quicksteps and waltzes there were occasional 'ladies' choices', so that unattached girls could get a dance by "buzzing off" the woman in the arms of a handsome man with the words, "Excuse me".

Occasionally, the romantic atmosphere was disturbed when fights broke out between rival families or as the result of "Town v. country" feuds; policemen generally waited outside to deal with anybody who was ejected. One night a one-legged man was so incensed that he used a crutch as a weapon, swinging it viciously at anybody who approached. If Guy Fawkes night happened to fall on a Saturday, the throwing of fireworks could get out of hand, forcing the band to abandon proceedings before the normal time.

There were also frivolous incidents to enliven the "bob hops". As the dancers dispersed after a quickstep, a pair of ladies' panties was spotted in the middle of the dance floor. Stunned silence gave way to prolonged laughter. Eventually, a brave young man picked up the knickers and threw them on the stage. The owner's secret was never revealed.

As well as leading the Melody Makers on Saturday evenings, Frank Walton contributed to Penrith's dancing years by bringing several bands of national repute to the Drill Hall. A traditional ball, with Harry Davidson and his orchestra, sparked a revival of old-time dancing in town. Harry Gold and his Pieces of Eight, the Sid Phillips band and the Charles Amer orchestra, from Butlin's holiday camp, Filey, all pulled in the crowds. The pop era was heralded by a visit by Rue and the Rockets.

Hunt balls, marathon jives and beauty contests were all part of the Drill Hall dance scene. Lilian Bond, a lovely, dark-haired girl who worked at the Beechwood milkbar, became the first post-war "Miss Penrith", and Sheila Robertson, a 15-year-old shop assistant, was adjudged the town's "personality girl", both over half-a-century ago.

Although the Drill Hall is now remembered primarily for the Saturday night "bob hops", the history of dancing there stretched back into the 1800's. In 1897 the *Cumberland and Westmorland Advertiser* reported: "On Thursday the Penrith Drill and Concert Hall presented a most brilliant and captivating appearance on the occasion of Mrs. Riley of Ennim having sent out invitations to a large circle of friends to attend a ball."

The hall was transformed to provide a gentlemen's smoke room and lounge, a ladies' boudoir and a dainty tea-room. Hundreds of coloured lights, suspended baskets of flowers and large mirrors, draped with lace curtains, all contributed to the air of splendour. Herr Iff's orchestra, from Glasgow, was engaged and played up-to-the-minute numbers like *The Circus Girl*, *The Liberty Belle* and *Chin Chin Chinaman*.

Entertainers who graced the hall in its early days included Charles Coburn, who became famous for the popular song, *The man who broke the bank at Monte Carlo*.

Originally built by public subscription for £3,000 and administered by trustees, the hall was sold to the War Office in 1913 to provide headquarters for the Territorial Army, but this did not prevent townsfolk from using it for social functions, political meetings, presentations by Penrith Players and other events, although sentimentalists tend to think mainly of their dancing years in the hall. Then, sadly and suddenly, the heart of Penrith's community life stopped beating ...

The 20th February 1963 was one of the coldest days of the year, with 19 degrees of frost. At 2-45 in the morning the Drill Hall was seen to be on fire. Firemen were quickly on the scene – the fire sta-

Whilst turning hay in a field close to the Penrith Beacon, this farmer could enjoy views over the old sandstone town, in the direction of Ullswater.

tion was then only a stone's throw away, at the other end of Portland Place – only to discover that the main water supply had been turned off as a precaution during the freeze-up.

Things went from bad to worse, for the water manager, who lived nearby, could not be roused for some time and an hour passed before the water began to flow. The delay was fatal to the Drill Hall and Penrithians, going to work next morning, were greeted by the sight of the famous building in a sorrowful state, with half the roof destroyed, glass, plaster and timber littering the ground and the dance floor awash with water.

A housewife, in a letter to the *Herald*, voiced her concern at the practice of turning off the water supply in the depths of winter. She said: "In the past we were told that the water would be turned on again immediately if there was a fire in the town. But the other night it was proved that this is not the case.

"For an hour, frightened people were forced to watch a fire at the Drill Hall threatening their homes, while firemen and police stood out in bitter cold, helpless because no water was coming through the hoses. Suppose the wind had been blowing hard that night."

There may have been happy memories of the Drill Hall but it was allowed to slip away with scarcely a word of protest. Although there were bound to be thoughts of acquiring the property for the town when the local Territorial Association announced its intention to dispose of the fire-ravaged shell, councillors seemingly considered the buying of the premises, plus the restoration or adaptation and the long-term question of upkeep, to be too formidable a proposition.

And, to be fair to the local authority, there were no letters in the press suggesting that the damaged building should be bought from the War Office. The *Herald* itself spoke of such a venture as "fantastically expensive" and posed the question, "In any case, is there any substantial demand for such a hall in these days of ubiquitous TV?"

The end came in April 1965, the *Herald* reporting: "There can now be no reprieve for the 70-year-old Penrith Drill Hall. Contractors began work on its demolition two weeks ago but this week the first visible effects became evident as the outer walls were knocked down. For many years the town's great social and recreational centre, the Drill Hall is being knocked down to make way for a new block of Crown Offices."

So the town lost its beloved Drill Hall, but another famous building of the 1890s, the former Jubilee Cottage Hospital, on the Beacon Edge, lives on, albeit in a different guise. It has been converted into flats since the closure of the hospital in 1987.

It was the Victorians who, by their initiative and industry, provided Penrith with the "Cottage" as a means of marking the diamond jubilee of Queen Victoria in 1897. For many years, up to the setting up of the National Health Service, Penrith people – and Penrith people alone – sat on committees which ran the hospital, keeping a close eye on finances and making staff appointments.

Most townsfolk visited the "Cottage" at some time after a slight mishap – perhaps a sprained wrist, that rather nasty cut near an eye after tumbling in the playground at school, a non-stop nosebleed or the painful day when a small boy on a sledge had an ear bitten by a

Old folk of Penrith enjoy a free meal in the Drill Hall, the town's premier social centre for more than 60 years. Below: the sad scene after fire swept through the hall in the 1960s, leading to its demolition. *(Alec Fraser)*

passing Labrador dog. For others, the hospital held (and still holds) poignant memories of the final days and hours of a loved one – memories of care, consideration and devotion on the part of the nursing staff.

Community life suffered a double blow in the mid-1960s. While the town was still pondering over the impending fate of the fire-damaged Drill Hall, news broke of a threat to another precious institution.

"See you at the 'YM'," was a call heard frequently among youngsters. The Penrith Young Men's Christian Association, housed in a substantial sandstone building at the bottom of Sandgate, was a gathering ground for teenage boys and men in their early twenties. Quite simply, it was "somewhere to go", either to chat with contemporaries or to play table tennis, snooker or billiards. There was nothing elaborate about the place but it was available to youngsters who might otherwise have hung about on the street corners or made a nuisance of themselves. What was more appealing to them was the fact that the YMCA was free from officialdom or rigid control.

It would be an exaggeration to suggest that all the young members were angelic characters, incapable of misconduct, but the "YM" was such a boon to them that they seldom, if ever, kicked over the traces by abusing the building or the facilities.

Remarkably, the officials of the immediate post-war years – men like Eddie Allen, George Bowman and Cliff Sisson – were unpaid volunteers. They engaged a caretaker to run the building but often called to keep a friendly eye on day-to-day activities, as well as running football and cricket teams for seniors and juniors on Saturdays.

Dancing classes, Sunday evening meetings, which were addressed by local celebrities, and occasional outings to Morecambe by motor coach, with girlfriends invited, were also on the YMCA programme. The youth of Penrith prospered and men now in their 60s and 70s must realise how lucky they were – although at the time they probably took it all for granted.

The "YM" I remember was such a vibrant organisation that a fatal decline seemed unlikely, if not impossible. The decision to appoint a full-time leader, and the resultant expenditure, have been blamed, but the reasons were probably more complex. Certainly, fortunes seemed to fade after an enforced move from the Sandgate building (later demolished) to less auspicious premises in Victoria Road. Crisis-point was reached when another change of headquarters became necessary and the YMCA had an overdraft of just over £1,000.

Hopes were briefly revived at a packed meeting in the Town Hall, presided over by the Earl of Lonsdale. The strength of local opinion seemed to put beyond doubt the town's support for its 80-year-old YMCA, prompting the chairman, Jim Harrison, to say: "I believe Penrith is going to show its young citizens what public and Christian spirit can do for them."

Alas, it was not to be; strong words were not matched by positive action. The vicar of Penrith, Canon Richard Bradford, spoke of his sadness and pleaded, "We need half-a-dozen mature men and women willing to give themselves to the service of our young people." Nobody answered the call and the fade-out continued. Even now, over 30 years later, consciences must be troubled whenever the halcyon days of Penrith YMCA are recalled.

The choicest, most-sought-after seats in town are in the twin bay windows of the George Hotel, fronting on to Devonshire Street, a vital, invariably crowded thoroughfare, with a constant flow of traffic and people. If you manage to get one of the window seats at coffee time, you have a front row view of the town at work and play – strolling pensioners, scuttling shoppers and slow-motion sightseers. Deep in history this was the place to be, for stagecoaches and mail coaches pulled up in the street outside the hotel with a clatter of hooves and a "Ta-ra-ra" of the guard's horn.

The heart of local life has always beat strongly at the George (though it once shared the limelight with the now-demolished Crown Hotel, some 400 yards to the south on the main street). Top tittle-tattlers and friendly socialisers get together to give the coffee room a vitality which rises and falls according to the time of day and the prevailing weather.

Lives, loves and reputations are high on the mid-morning menu to be relished with coffee and biscuits, tea and toast, gin and tonic, whisky and lemonade.

Socialising is not confined to coffee time at the George or some other place of refreshment. Club life flourishes in the hotel.

Mondays see the weekly luncheons of the Rotary Club which has a proud record of service to the community, stretching over half-a-century and including the creation of a much-used garden of rest near the parish church and the opening of an Abbeyfield home, for elderly people, in a former maternity hospital.

The lunches provide a convivial break in the weekly slog for bank managers, accountants, senior police officers, farmers, shopkeepers and other professional or businessmen. They may be called on to pay "fines", for charity, if they wear gaudy ties or racy braces, boast new cars or pictures in the local paper or commit some light-hearted misdemeanour.

Rotary figures in the pedigrees of other clubs, such as Inner Wheel (made up of Rotarians' wives), Round Table (for younger men) and Probus (for more elderly men). Add to the tally the Soroptimists (another ladies' group) and the Lions Club (a men's organisation with headquarters at the George) and you have an impression of club life in a small town.

The town as a whole has derived a lot of benefit from these chummy organisations. The Lions' contributions to communal pride include the arranging of the annual May Day carnival, with marching bands, colourful and imaginative floats, excited children and proud parents, dancers, merry-go-rounds, sideshows and hot dogs. Much of the work is less eyecatching, such as the Soroptimists' campaigns, one to raise awareness of the drugs problem and another to highlight the threats faced by women alone in the streets.

Everybody has a miscellany of memories concerning buildings. Some make a firmer imprint on the memory than others. A painful recollection relates to the former Penrith Boys' Council School, now an annexe to the Queen Elizabeth Grammar School which is almost next-door in Ullswater Road.

My teacher asked me to take the headmaster's tea to his office. As I mounted the steep stairs, I was aware that the cup was wobbling on the saucer, so applied my right thumb to the rim to avoid any spillage. The head, waiting at the office door, spotted the offending thumb immediately.

"Boy," he snapped. "I told you yesterday not to put your dirty thumb in my tea. Hold your hand out."

My muttered plea that it was the first time I had performed the duty fell on deaf ears. The head's cane crashed down twice on my trembling mitt.

Canes swished with some frequency at the Boys' Council in the 1930s, generally with greater justification than on that occasion outside the head's office. Allegations of inattentiveness, smudges on exercise books and unwarranted noises in the classroom were punished swiftly and effectively. If a fearful pupil pulled back his hand as the cane was brought down, skilled swishers showed no mercy; with lightning speed the supple weapon was put into reverse, so that it caught the offender across the knuckles, causing even greater pain.

The cane was seen as an aid to learning and the passing of exams. It was an extreme view – but the school could point to an impressive record of success in preparing boys for the grammar school.

The Musgrave Monument is at the very heart of Penrith – a clock tower photographed more than any other feature, seen by every traveller who drives through the town centre and revered by the locals. It has survived several threats in its life of 140 years, mainly for road safety reasons. As far back as 1931 a guest speaker at the chamber of trade's dinner had the impudence to suggest that the Monument should be scrapped, claiming that it was an obstruction to cars which were "scorching" through town at 25 mph!

The depth of sentimental feeling about the classic landmark surfaced again in 1997 because of a contentious plan to marginalise the Monument by altering the easy-to-negotiate northbound traffic flow, to the west, to a sharp left-hand turn round the opposite side. The fear was that heavy vehicles might strike the stonework in making the turn or weaken the ancient foundations, on account of increased vibrations.

The town rose in opposition to the council-backed plan, which had been designed to "calm" traffic. Any threat to a beloved piece of Penrith must be resisted – vehemently. There followed a council-organised referendum on an alternative plan, to move the tower a short distance – but that was also dismissed by the power and passion of public opinion.

The Monument was built in 1861 to the memory of a member of the local gentry, Philip Musgrave, who had died two years earlier in

Madrid, and as a tribute to Sir George and Lady Musgrave. They lived at Eden Hall, a mansion a few miles to the east of town, later to be demolished.

Frankly, however, the origins of the clock tower matter little. Penrithians see it through emotional eyes – the spot where, by tradition, generations have gathered to celebrate in unison. For example, they were there to make merry in marking the Reliefs of Mafeking and Ladysmith, and then to celebrate the end of the Boer war in South Africa where volunteers from Penrith had been fighting.

And on 11th November of 1918, when the Great War ended, the town crier summoned Penrith people to the same place. Tom Smith, as chairman of the urban council, spoke of the town's loss of 150 men who would not return from the battlefront, the national anthem was sung and a fat heifer was roasted for public consumption!

Many years later, as the war of 1939-45 ended, inhabitants headed automatically to the Monument. Hundreds of couples waltzed and quickstepped in the street to amplified music from a shop window, on VE and VJ nights. "Thunderflashes", powerful fireworks brought into town by soldiers stationed at nearby Army camps, occasionally exploded and scattered the jubilant dancers. The Monument is seen as essential. Without it, Penrith simply wouldn't be Penrith.

16

A look at the paper

It's breakfast-time on Saturday morning in Penrith and district. There's little doubt that the question heard most frequently, as the tea, toast and marmalade are consumed, is: "Owt in the *Herald* this week?"

And so it has been over a wide area of Cumbria for 140 years, ever since the paper was first published, under the title of *Penrith Herald*. Thirty years later, the original masthead was displaced by the less memorable *Mid-Cumberland and North Westmorland Herald*, and in 1926 the present name, *Cumberland and Westmorland Herald*, was adopted.

In one sense, there is nothing completely new in the *Herald*; much that it reports has happened before, albeit to other characters in different locations and with slight variations in fine details. By their very nature, weekly papers are repetitious and cover the same events, year after year – sports days, May days, rushbearings, agricultural shows, flower shows, annual meetings and many more.

Glance at an old paper, with the dateline erased, and you can probably tell the time of year by some of the principal reports. If Threlkeld and Patterdale "dog days", Skelton show and Grasmere sports are covered, the month is August; if the big sheep sales at Lazonby hit the headlines, then it's September. Turn to the advertising pages and the public notices about Christmas domino drives and whist drives give evidence of the approach of the festive season.

The *Herald* is the proud survivor out of three Penrith newspapers, all launched within a few years of each other. The *Cumberland and Westmorland Advertiser* was the first on the scene, in 1855; the *Herald* and the *Penrith Observer* followed five years later.

In the first issue of the *Herald*, dated 17th November 1860, the founder-editor, Thomas Hodgson, wrote: "In these days of universal reading and writing a demand has sprung up in our neighbourhood for a weekly newspaper that will circulate at a cheap price, that will offer our advertising friends a suitable medium, which will let us know what each is doing and what is doing in England and abroad."

Journalists today can only imagine the competitive spirit which drove on their forebears long ago. The three rival papers struggled for survival until the close of the 19th Century when the *Advertiser* became the first to feel the pressure. In a desperate bid, the paper altered its name to *Penrith Times* and switched its day of publication from Tuesday to Saturday, so that it was in more direct opposition to the *Herald*.

Those must have been anxious times for *Herald* workers. In fact, the editor, Thomas Hodgson, walked up to the railway station every Friday evening to count the bundles of the rival papers which were awaiting despatch to Keswick and up the Eden Valley.

Directors, journalists, printers and advertisement staff of the Herald in the newspapers's centenary year, 1960.

The *Penrith Times* quickly folded, leaving the field to the *Herald* on Saturdays and the *Penrith Observer* on Tuesdays, a situation which persisted until 1968 when, sadly, sagging circulation figures and advertising revenue put an end to the *Observer*. Tuesdays were never quite the same again.

Newspapermen are not the hard-bitten characters of films and fiction. Rival reporters are also their friends and the loss of any paper is a matter for regret. Although a newspaper 'war' had been won, the *Herald* would miss the spur of having to keep ahead of a worthy competitor.

In its early years the *Herald* was a fascinating mixture of parochial paragraphs with national and international news, for few people could afford daily newspapers in those distant days. Half a page was devoted to the weekly instalment of a romantic novel, such as *Leonora's Legacy, Vengeance is mine* or *The Captain's Daughter*, while another column was made up of juvenile items "for the little folk". A "ladies' letter" provided a rich mixture of hints on dress, society gossip, advice on how to care for the skin and recipes for Venus pudding and Devonshire junket.

Farmers' wives in the Eden Valley must have been enthralled to learn that a Parisian dressmaker had just completed a marvellous ball gown for the Duchess of Leuchtenberg. There was a weekly column of news from the House of Commons and, for the benefit of sports enthusiasts, the local cricket scores were sometimes embellished by word of the latest feats of W.G. Grace at Lord's. Spice was added by frequent reports of divorce and breach of promise cases under headlines which simply couldn't be ignored, such as "A jilted widow" and "The clergyman's romance".

But the backbone of the *Herald*, then as now, was local news. Police courts and Board of Health deliberations used to be covered in strict chronological order, rather than on news merit, invariably commencing with lists of the JPs and councillors in attendance. Shorter items described happenings as diverse as kern suppers, old penny pitching challenges, soup kitchens for poor people, temperance meetings, obituary tributes, the arrival of Lord Lonsdale for the grouse shooting and a rich variety of others.

Newspaper production relies on a range of talents, skills and endeavours, on the constant co-operation of printers and advertising people, and on the enthusiasm and motivation of reporters and photographers who are the eyes and ears of any news publication.

But the *Herald* also depends heavily on the goodwill of men and women in towns and villages who see the newspaper as *theirs* and maintain a regular supply of news items, information and ideas. New vogues in journalism tend to downgrade such contributions as parish pump news – a lesser form of content – when, in fact, they are the lifeblood of papers like the *Herald*.

People in remote places relish the news of who heard the first cuckoo, caught a monster trout or salmon, dug up a gigantic potato, found a Roman coin while tending the garden, or of old schoolfriends meeting up accidentally after half-a-century.

To work on national dailies is seen as the goal of newspapermen but many ex-reporters feel privileged to have spent a long career away from the clamour and the glamour of the big city. I have precious memories of days spent in the Cumbrian countryside, covering May days, garden parties and shows. The sporting scene has also been rich and varied, with its outspoken football fans, the comparative quietude of delectable cricket grounds, village sports in farmers' fields and the annual spectacle of "Glorious Grasmere", mecca of wrestlers, fell runners and the hound trailing fraternity in a matchless setting.

"A suitable medium" for advertisers was promised by the paper's pioneer in 1860. In fact, advertisements hold more appeal for readers than newspapermen like to admit – and many years ago they were a source of much amusement, as well as information.

The curative properties of a certain brand of pills were once presented in the style of a news item with arresting headlines: "Snatched from death ... working girl's miraculous recovery from heart disease, dropsy, indigestion and neuralgia ... ten doctors attended and an infirmary staff failed to relieve her ... her grave clothes were prepared and the bearers selected ..."

It was a harrowing account of a young woman in a Yorkshire town who was "saved from the grave" by a box of pills costing a mere 1s. 1½d. (about 7 pence in today's coinage). The story of her miraculous recovery was reinforced by sworn statements by neighbours.

Some potions, costing only a few pence, were said to cure almost every known ailment. Scores of Penrith-area people, who suffered from bad backs, giddiness and shooting pains in the loins, found that spending 2s. 9d. on a box of backache pills was an unbeatable investment, and their letters of praise appeared in the *Herald* in the form of articles-cum-advertisements.

'Aspro' adopted a similar policy in the 1930s, printing effusive letters from satisfied customers. "I feel it is my duty to write to you about the benefit I have derived from your wonderful tablets. They have been a godsend to me," wrote J.B. from the Wirral. Pictures of smiling women and gargling men stressed the effectiveness of the cure which, in those days, could be bought for as little as threepence in old coinage.

Another gem of persuasive advertising, of older vintage, claimed that nightlights – only a shilling apiece in price – were a sure safeguard against crime. Described in the blurb as the "burglar's horror", they were said to be recommended by the police as a deterrent to nocturnal intruders. To press home this wise counsel, there was a striking picture of a burglar confronted by a belligerent-looking old woman in a nightcap, holding a nightlight in one hand and a poker in the other. Bill Sykes, obviously shaken to the core, recoiled in dismay, while his jemmy and bludgeon fell from nerveless fingers.

Although the *Herald* news columns were free from any hint of salaciousness, the underwear adverts were slightly risqué, embodying drawings of solemn-looking, middle-aged women gazing earnestly into space as they stood about in girdles. "A corset for every figure," said John H. Howe, Penrith, in advertising Twilfit Corsetry. "A price for every purse".

Looked at in retrospect, the corsetry adverts of the inter-war years suggest heavyweight upholstery and foundation garments which were as grotesque as they were unglamorous. High-tech fibres have revolutionised women's tummy-flattening garments, but there is no doubt that old-fashioned corsets and the hose-supporting appendages were seen as the embodiment or style and sexual appeal by our grandmothers and great-grandmothers. Doubtless, their menfolk also studied the adverts.

Public notices reflected (and still reflect) the community spirit in towns and villages – the fetes, WI bazaars, children's sports and fancy dress parades; even the smallest village boasted at least one "do" every summer. Parochial sales of work were cheek by jowl with missionary sales, folk dance festi-

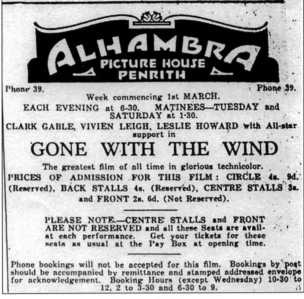

Cinema adverts were read avidly. The Penrith Alhambra showed a famous film in 1943.

vals with three-act plays, athletic sports with charity balls and flannel dances.

Threlkeld sheepdog trials would take place "wet or fine" and the "world-famed" Grasmere sports were said to be "under Royal patronage".

People become addicted to weekly newspapers, just as they do to brands of coffee and types of breakfast cereal. It is a proprietorial kind of attachment, for long-established readers note and comment on changes in style and presentation, sometimes critically. What the journalist sees as an improvement to the paper may be viewed by the readership as a break with tradition.

Misprints, which can elude the proof readers in the early stages of publication, seem to leap from the page as soon as the paper is printed – and it's too late to make a correction. Such errors in printing are often the delight of keen-eyed readers and the curse of editors. The *Herald* must have admitted to many little mistakes over the years, the most disastrous occurring in a leader written in the days of Gladstone's Government in the 19th Century. A sentence

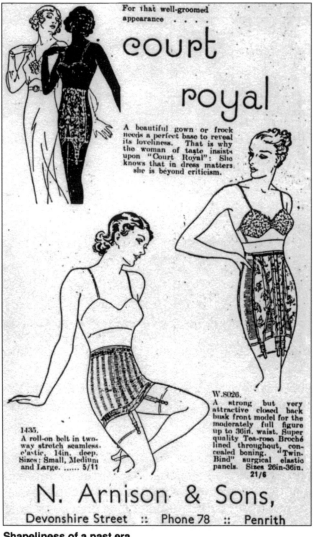

For that well-groomed appearance . . . .

court

royal

A beautiful gown or frock needs a perfect base to reveal its loveliness. That is why the woman of taste insists upon "Court Royal": She knows that in dress matters she is beyond criticism.

1435.
A roll-on belt in two-way stretch seamless, elastic. 14in. deep. Sizes: Small, Medium and Large. 5/11

W.8026.
A strong but very attractive closed back busk front model for the moderately full figure up to 36in. waist. Super quality Tea-rose Broché lined throughout, concealed boning. "Twin-Bind" surgical elastic panels. Sizes 26in-36in. 21/6

N. Arnison & Sons,
Devonshire Street :: Phone 78 :: Penrith

Shapeliness of a past era . . .

was meant to begin, "When Mr. Gladstone has cleared the encumbrances from the ground he will ... "

Alas, the printer mistook the word "encumbrances" for "cucumbers" – and so it appeared in the *Herald*.

If the weekly paper is to be a reflection of the area which it serves, it must not only report the day-to-day happenings but, also, mirror all the changes and trends affecting the lives of local folk. Enthusiasms must be shared, anxieties aired, successes extolled and major proposals and developments perused. When views clash, both sides must be represented in the coverage; balance is paramount.

In essence, the files of the *Herald* make up a massive history book. Its 140 years began in the horsedrawn era, for founder-editor Thomas Hodgson travelled to Penrith by stagecoach from his native town of Barnard Castle, as he set out on his career in newspapers.

The coach rumbled to a halt at the George Hotel which, in later years – 1897, to be precise – saw a great stir with the arrival of an autocar. Mr. H. Sturmey, Coventry, the driver, was en route from John O'Groats to Land's End. The Earl of Lonsdale, of Lowther Castle, commented: "I don't think motor cars will interfere with coaching, at least not from the point of view of sport. I believe the talk about the extinction of coaches and horses is nonsense."

Down the years, all the aspects of travel have been covered: The first "speeding" motor cars, checked with stop watches in the streets of Penrith at 12 mph ... pioneer bus proprietors like Ernie Hartness whose lorry-cum-bus took farmers' wives to market with eggs, poultry and butter ... heavy lorries grinding over Shap Fell on the A6 ... the building of the M6 motorway ... the decline and fall of local rail services, except for the visually delightful Settle-Carlisle line which was saved after an epic struggle.

As in the case of travel, agriculture, electrification, industry in its many forms, tourism, local government, sport and leisure activity have all changed immeasurably over the years and few details of their countless developments have not been recorded in the weekly paper.

Essentially, however, local papers are about local people. Human lives can be charted within the pages of the *Herald*, beginning with a notice of birth, continuing with school successes and then, possibly, a marriage notice or report, career appointments and advances, club memberships and sporting feats, a retirement party, a wedding anniversary and then the finality of the obituary tribute.

Not all individuals will receive such generous treatment but, from time to time, there are personal details of most folk, all keenly read by friends, acquaintances and neighbours. So are the 'juicier' details of follies or misdeeds in the event of a court appearance by a well-known person.

Progress in the presentation of news has gathered pace and style during the lifetime of the Penrith paper, with many pictures and some advertisements now in colour. In another advance of the 1990s, the *Herald* has a website, so that users of Internet worldwide can pick up a resumé of Eden's top news stories, vintage pictures and the "Looking Backwards" column – at the touch of a button.

17

Rural routes

Many moons ago, there was a time when the village railway station, on the country or branch line, was an integral part of rural England. Colourful flower beds, a neat office and spotlessly clean waiting room, all zealously cared for, were a joy to behold and business was brisk. Alas, the glory of the small stations has gone and, in the case of Eden, three out of four country railways have disappeared.

There was a homespun charm about the old stations. As a steam train drew alongside one of the platforms on the former Eden Valley line, the welcoming cry was brief but distinctive: "WarCOP ... WarCOP ... WarCOP".

The emphasis placed on the second syllable, with great relish, by the stationmaster at Warcop, remains an endearing memory of a rail service that is no more.

Closure of the Eden Valley service, first predicted in 1959, prompted double-pronged opposition because it was announced at the same time as the proposed shutdown of another old-timer, the Cockermouth, Keswick and Penrith line. Both had terminals at Penrith, thereby combining to provide a valued link between the industrialised North-East and the tourism-dependent Lake District and, in particular, the holiday town of Keswick.

The campaign to preserve the Eden Valley involved a variety of concerned Cumbrians – MPs, councillors, hoteliers and others of the catering industry – supported by traditionalists with memories of picturesque times when the line was abustle with the sight and sound of smart, green-liveried engines, embellished with gleaming brasswork. They stood in a bay at Penrith station, hissing or throbbing as the case might be. The steam whistle blew – or, in later years, the horn of the diesel gave a tuneful toot – as the wheels began to turn on the 60-mile run to Darlington.

The highlight for many passengers was the crossing of the Belah Viaduct, six miles east of Kirkby Stephen. Over 1,000 feet long and consisting of a lattice girder superstructure of wrought iron, with abutments and foundations of stone, the spectacular viaduct was designed by Sir Thomas Bouch, who was also the designer of the ill-fated bridge over the river Tay in Scotland. The Tay bridge was opened in 1877 but collapsed two years later as a train was crossing on a stormy night, with the loss of about 80 lives.

During the construction of Belah viaduct, completed in 43 days at a cost of £31,630, a document was placed in one of the columns, giving the main dimensions and ending with a verse:

> To future ages these lines will tell
> Who built this structure o'er the dell.
> Gilkes Wilson with these eighty men
> Raised Belah's viaduct o'er the glen.

For more than a century the viaduct withstood the wind and the weather of the Pennine uplands, carrying thousands of trains, until its fate was sealed by an economy drive by the railway authorities.

The anti-closure campaign was enlivened when an Eden businessman claimed that he could do a better job than British Railways in running the line. "I would like the opportunity of taking over the line," said Watson Sayer in a letter to BR. "I am prepared to rent the line for a period of one year, with an option to renew at the end of the year."

Mr. Sayer, a Kirkby Stephen man of many involvements – haulier, quarry owner, cafe proprietor and garage owner – had a reputation for getting into the news headlines. He once received national publicity for his tactics in trying to save a garage sign from demolition. The sign did not have planning permission and when council workmen were sent to remove it, "Watty" Sayer tried to fend them off by attaching a Shorthorn bull!

Although his offer to run the railway line was rejected, Mr. Sayer fought on and was a member of a seven-man delegation sent to London in 1961 to meet BR chiefs. Spirits rose in the valley when a reprieve was granted – but the finale was merely being delayed.

Two "last" trains ran on the evening of 20th January 1962. The final train of the normal diesel service was sent on its way by a whistle blown by Kenneth Jones, as chairman of Penrith Urban Council, followed soon afterwards by the last train of all, nine coaches carrying 440 rail enthusiasts and drawn by a steam engine, as the first one had been a century earlier.

Mourners gathered along the route to watch and to condemn. The chairman of Kirkby Stephen Parish Council, Mr. F. William Parrott, said that it was "an act of incredible stupidity" to close a trans-country line which linked three main lines and passed through country of great charm. It was a day of immense sadness at Kirkby Stephen, for almost 200 local men once worked on the railway but, after the axe fell, only a handful remained in the deserted and desolate station.

There was a sociable feeling about the old Cockermouth, Keswick and Penrith line and about the little stations along the route, at Blencowe, Penruddock, Troutbeck and Threlkeld. Farmers' wives used the service to take butter and eggs to market, while insurance agents and other country travellers put their pushbikes in the guard's van, getting off at one of the stations to make calls in remote places. Non-corridor trains ran on the old CK and P line, leading to an alternative interpretation of the initials as "Carriage Kissing Prohibited".

Train spotters recorded stately steam trains, described as "Cauliflowers" and "Jumbos", before nippy diesels took over from steam in 1955.

The existence of a station at Troutbeck, midway between Penrith and Keswick, was a factor in the development of an auction mart for the sale of sheep from fellside farms. In turn, the mart boosted the nearby Troutbeck Hotel, where hungry farmers relished lashings of ham and eggs and big helpings of tatie pot. The mart survived the closure of the railway line until 1991 when the auctioneers' monotonous chatter was heard for the last time.

The campaign to retain the line was strongest in Keswick, a town heavily dependent on holidaymakers. A leading townsman, Sir Percy Hope, said that closure would be "a disaster too dreadful to contemplate". The truth was that, with most visitors preferring the

Sweet music flowed from a railway signalbox at Penrith in days long past, for signalman Charlie Rae whiled away the time between trains by playing his violin, to the amusement of the "box boy", Ken Harper. *(Alec Fraser)*

greater convenience of car travel, the line could no longer pay its way.

A chapter of rail history stretching back 108 years closed on 4th March 1972 as the last train for Keswick set out from Penrith to the strains of "Auld Lang Syne", played by the town band. More than 400 enthusiasts collected memorabilia and the autograph of train driver John Fordham. Charles Arnison, a Penrith solicitor, wore clogs, as he associated the clatter of porters' clogs on the platform with his earliest memories of making the journey. As the train raced into the night on the return trip, Norman Beanland, a Keswick councillor, suggested that the old line might "live again" under the auspices of rail buffs. His words have echoed down the years...

The closure of the Eden Valley railway line in 1962 was a sad day for the town of Appleby whose Mayor, James Whitehead, shook hands with the driver of the last train.

The lure of the steam train is infectious and incurable – and the Pennine town of Alston has cashed in on this addiction. When its rail link with Haltwhistle, and the wider world beyond, was lost, the South Tynedale Railway Preservation Society stepped in and turned the discarded station, the unwanted route and some magnificent countryside into a narrow guage railway on which visitors can make a short journey along the banks of the Tyne to Kirkhaugh, beyond the border with Northumbria. Enthusiasm for steam trains has become a boost to the economy of Alston.

The sole survivor among Eden's country railways is the Settle-Carlisle, which runs through the Eden Valley and the Yorkshire Dales, a picture-postcard route abounding in tunnels and viaducts. But by 1983 neither British Rail nor the Government thought the line was worthy of preservation. Environment secretary Nicholas Ridley aroused passions by claiming that local folk using the line could be fitted into a decent mini-bus, with seats to spare. "It is entirely for its scenic and touristic value that many people want to see the railway kept open," he added.

Northerners were angry at the threat to an essential service for those living in remote places, a lifeline which could be the key to future developments. They blamed the north-south "divide" for the fact that they did not have a fair share of the nation's resources. Under mounting pressure from local authorities, a supportive press and the rail buffs of the "Friends of the Settle-Carlisle line", the Government finally retreated from the long-held view that the line had no effective future.

The saving of the Settle-Carlisle, announced in 1989, was a victory for public opinion over the massed ranks of British Rail and politicians. The line would now be dead but for a sustained showing of northern spirit.

While rail services have diminished, the roadways of Eden have progressed spectacularly since the days of the old-time toll bars, on the approaches to Penrith and other towns, where travellers paid over pence for themselves, their vehicles and any animals they might have.

The bypass of Penrith was mooted in the 1930s but a kind of road-building paralysis set in, due partly to the second war. By the time the first sods were cut in 1965, the original plan for a short relief road had grown into something much grander – the Penrith section of the M6, an extension of the motorway system into the heart of the north of England, built at a cost of £10 million.

There was another price to pay, for the lush beauty of farm fields and hedges, and the idyllic walks which crossed them, had to be swept aside to provide the vast commuting tracks, on which drivers would neither know nor care about the countryside they were passing through. Travel between towns and cities would become like some timeless, dateless film, without any sense of place or history.

That said, by the time the bypass was opened in 1968, motorways had become essential – vital arteries offering fast, safe travel over long hauls. As Robert Brown, the joint parliamentary secretary to the Ministry of Transport, snipped a white ribbon, he commented that Penrith should be "a quieter, better place to live in". It

Rural bliss was replaced by the continual roar of heavy traffic when Penrith was bypassed by a section of the M6 in the late-1960s. The fields to the west of town began to change when workmen removed the first turf from the agreed route. Three years later, the Penrith bypass was opened.

would be recognised again for its own sake and not just as a traffic snarl on the A6.

These are momentous times, with many technological advances, but the price of progress is the loss of much that is old and out-of-date, yet nostalgic and wonderful. In Eden, at least, we can still stop and stare – and remember.

Index of place names

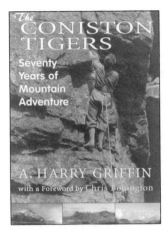
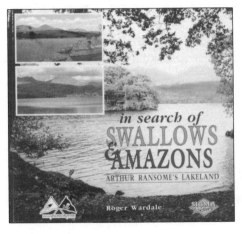